extra credit

An Almanac
of
Thinking Activities

by Nancy Polette

Pieces of Learning

© 2000 Nancy Polette
Published by Pieces of Learning
1990 Market Road
Marion IL 62959
polmarion@midamer.net
www.piecesoflearning.com
CLC0250
ISBN 1-880505-89-4
Printed in the U.S.A.

September 1

Beginning of World War II

On September 1, 1939, Germany invaded Poland, setting off a conflict that would involve all the nations of the world. Choose one year during World War II (1939-1945).
Use an almanac to **answer these questions** about the year you chose.
1. Who was President of the United States? _____
2. What was his political party? _____
3. Who was Vice President? _____
4. Who was Secretary of War? _____
5. Who was King of England? _____
6. Who won the Nobel Prize for Medicine? _____
7. Who won the Pulitzer Prize for fiction? _____
8. Who was Miss America? _____
9. What horse won the Kentucky Derby? _____
10. Who was the Pope? _____
11. Who won the World Series? _____
12. Who won the Academy Awards for best actor and best actress? _____

September 2

Great Fire in London 1666

This great fire destroyed more than 13,000 homes and 84 churches after breaking out in a baker's shop on Pudding Lane. It raged out of control for five days, but amazingly there were no deaths.
Three very good things happened as a result of this fire. Discover what they were. Read about the Great Fire and submit a **short report listing** the three benefits.

Benefits
1. _____

_____

2. _____

_____

3. _____

_____

September 3

First Professional Football Game 1895

Since this first game there have been many wacky and memorable moments in football history.

Using back issues of sports magazines and newspapers, create a **poster** of Memorable Moments in Football. Another good source of ideas is *Encyclopedia Brown's Book of Wacky Sports* by Donald Sobol. In this book you will read about the college game that had only one fan, the smallest football player ever and other wacky facts. In gathering information for your poster think about uniforms, players, skills, fans and teams.

September 4

Birthday of Syd Hoff 1912

Syd Hoff is well known for his "easy-to-read" books. He uses cartoon drawings to tell simple stories about animals. He often uses *alliteration* when writing about his characters. For example **D**anny meets a **d**inosaur and **S**lithers is a **s**nake.

Find at least one fact about each of these animals and write an **alliterative sentence** that includes the fact. Example: **R**attlesnakes **r**oam over **r**ough **r**ocks in desert **r**egions.

skunk   turtle   rabbit   snail   giraffe   kangaroo   polar bear   hyena

September 5

Birthday of Jesse James 1847-1882

Some say that Jesse James was a ruthless bandit. Others call him a modern day Robin Hood. Read about his life in the encyclopedia, on the Internet or in Margaret Baldwin's biography *Wanted: Frank and Jesse James* (Messner, 1981). Write a paragraph stating your **opinion**.

Here are other famous men of the 1800s. Place the names on a **chart** indicating which were lawmen, which were outlaws and which were both during their lives. **Draw** a tombstone for one of the men. Include an appropriate **epitaph**.

Wild Bill Hickok	Sam Bass	Roy Bean
Bat Masterson	Wyatt Earp	Tom Smith
Colt Younger	Billy the Kid	Charlie Siringo

September 6

Largest Kite Ever Flown

On this date in 1997 a kite that measured 10,043 square feet was flown for more than twenty minutes at the International Kite Festival in England.

Investigate the history of flight. Make a **time line** from man's earliest attempts to fly to modern day aviation. Be sure to include the following names in the correct order on your time line.

Glenn Curtis   Charles Lindbergh   Alan Shepard
Louis Berioz   The Wright Brothers

1700   2000

September 7

Birthday of Grandma Moses 1860-1961

This simple farm woman became one of the world's most well-known artists, yet she never had an art lesson. Read about her life in William Armstrong's biography *Barefoot In the Grass* or in another source. Use each of the words below in a separate **sentence to describe** a Moses characteristic or a situation in which she displayed that characteristic.

worried   unassuming   farsighted
grateful   eccentric   empathetic
inquisitive   tireless   dogmatic
dedicated   childlike   determined

September 8

Premier of *Star Trek* 1969

Many of the technologies shown on the early *Star Trek* shows seemed impossible in 1969. Consult *The Star Trek Concordance*, the Internet or other books about the show. **List** any of the seemingly impossible things shown in 1969 that are possible today.

Here are more life changes that scientists predict will happen in the next fifty years. Decide which are possible, probable and preferable. Choose one and write a short **essay** to defend your answer.

	Possible	Probable	Preferable
1. Education will take place totally at home through computers.	_____	_____	_____
2. Vacations can be taken in space.	_____	_____	_____
3. Artificial body parts will be available.	_____	_____	_____
4. The average life span will be 150 years.	_____	_____	_____
5. There will be mind travel rather than body travel to other places.	_____	_____	_____
6. Money will no longer change hands in business transactions.	_____	_____	_____
7. Operations will be performed by a doctor 1000s of miles away.	_____	_____	_____

September 9

National Grandparents Day

Interview your grandparents and/or older persons in the community. Ask each to give you a statement to be quoted concerning advice most needed for a young person facing a space age future.

Illustrate the quote and include a short **biography** of the person quoted.

Use *Bartlett's Quotations* to find a quote about the future that you believe will be helpful to young people. **Illustrate** this quote. Tell why you believe it is important, and include a short biography of the person whose words they are.

September 10

The Hot Dog Is Introduced

The first hot dog was introduced by Charles Feltman, a Coney Island baker, in 1919. Research the answer to these questions.

1. What do hot dogs contain? What do hamburgers contain?
2. Do hot dogs have nutritional value? Do hamburgers have nutritional value?

Prepare a **chart that compares** hot dogs and hamburgers for content, taste, nutritional value, cost, and types.

September 11

Birthday of William Sidney Porter (O. Henry) 1862-1910

O. Henry was a short story writer who was known as the master of the surprise ending. In *The Gift of the Magi* a husband sells his watch to buy beautiful combs for his wife's long hair. She sells her hair to buy a chain for his prized watch.

Write a story in O. Henry's style. Your characters are two kidnappers who take the young son of a rich businessman and ask for ransom for the child's return. At the end of your story the kidnappers are willing to pay the father to take the child back.

What will happen in the middle of the story?

September 12

Birthday of Jesse Owens 1913

This American athlete set world records in sprinting, hurdling, and jumping. In 1936 when the games were held in Germany he won the Olympic Medal in the 100 meter dash, the 200 meter dash, and the running broad jump.

While Hitler had made it a point to congratulate other Olympic winners, he turned his back on Jesse Owens and refused to acknowledge his accomplishments.

Read about Jesse Owen's life. If Jesse had written a letter to Hitler immediately after the 1936 Olympic Games what would he have written? Compose such a **letter**.

September 13

Highest Recorded Temperature 1922

Use an almanac to discover the highest temperature and where it occurred. Find a book about Global Warming or enter the topic Global Warming at this Internet site:
http://www.ajkids.com

Make a **chart** of the advantages and disadvantages of the entire world remaining at 80 degrees all the time.

September 14

Francis Scott Key Wrote The National Anthem 1812

Read about the history of the National Anthem in one of these books or in other reference sources in the library.

The Star Spangled Banner by Paul Galdone
Mr. Key's Song by Sadyebeth Lowitz
The Story of Fort McHenry and the Star Spangled Banner by Frederic Ray

Write and record a **news report** about the writing of "The Star Spangled Banner."
Present a dramatic reading of "The Star Spangled Banner" as if you were Francis Scott Key.

September 15

Birthday of Bruno Walter 1876-1962

Bruno Walter was a highly talented symphony and opera conductor. Many of his recordings are available for listening today. He was born in Berlin and at age 18 became the assistant conductor of the Hamburg Opera.

He came to the United States in 1939 and gained fame as the conductor of the New York Philharmonic and Metropolitan Opera orchestras.

He frequently conducted the works of a famous composer who was both a friend and teacher. **Name** this famous composer. **Play** part of one of his works for the class. Introduce the work by **telling** why it was written and what the composer hoped to achieve.

September 16

World Peace Day

The Nobel Peace Prize, established by Alfred Nobel, the inventor of dynamite, is given annually to the person or organization whose efforts have promoted world peace. Each person listed below has won the prize. **Identify** their contribution. Whose contribution do you feel will be the most lasting in achieving world peace? **Defend** your answer.

A. 1950 Ralph A. Bunche
B. 1952 Albert Schweitzer
C. 1962 Linus Pauling

D. 1972 Henry Kissinger
E. 1978 Anwar Sadat
F. 1979 Mother Theresa

September 17

Citizenship Day

This is a day set aside to reflect about what it means to be a citizen of a free nation. Find a copy of The Bill of Rights. **List** each of the rights and after each write an **explanation** of RESPONSIBILITIES we have as citizens to assure that these rights are enjoyed by all.

For example: The right to freedom of speech means that I am free to express my views on any topic, but I must also be **responsible** for not making untrue statements about others.

September 18

New York Times First Issue 1851

On this date, this famous newspaper which is still published today, came into being. Newspapers are an important part of our culture, allowing citizens not only to keep informed of the events of the day but to read varied opinions on important issues.

Choose an issue that is important to you. Sample topics might be recycling, world hunger, homeless people or defense of our country. Search your daily paper for one week and clip any pictures or articles about your topic. Arrange them as a **bulletin board display**. Make an attractive heading. Add other pictures or articles to the display as they appear in future editions of the newspaper.

September 19

Birthday of Rachel Field 1884-1942

In her award-winning book *Hitty: Her First Hundred Years* Rachel Field tells the story of the growth of the United States as seen through the eyes of a doll. To bring Hitty alive the author uses **personification**, a figure of speech in which an object displays human qualities.

Example:
I am a safety pin
Snuggling deep in a sewing box
Until reaching fingers grasp and squeeze
My slender frame.
My cousins are needles and pins that
Vacation in odd places when needed.
I dance to a beat with the shirt that holds me,
Perfect partners.

Choose an object to **write** about.
What human qualities can you give it?
Think about where it might live,
what work it does that people do,
what relatives it might have, where it
would take a holiday, how it is dressed
and how it moves.
Share your **poem** with the class.

September 20

Magellan Begins His Search for the Passage to India 1519

Research Magellan's trip and keep a **log** as Magellan did when aboard ship. Record daily events for seven days. At the end of seven days, choose one event from each day to **illustrate** on a **time line**. For each illustration, write a **sentence describing** the event and include what day is being shown. Include all seven days of your log on the time line.

September 21

Hawaii Joined the Union 1959

Make a Hawaii **scrapbook** titled *Hawaii Is...* On each page describe one thing that is always associated with Hawaii. For example: Hawaii is islands, Hawaii is volcanoes, Hawaii is leis. Give factual information about the item, provide an illustration and write a short poem.

For a good example see *A New England Scrapbook* by Loretta Krupinski.

September 22

Birthday of The Earl of Chesterfield 1694-1773

This English aristocrat is remembered for the four hundred letters he wrote to his son, Philip, over a thirty year period. His letters were intended to give Philip advice in manners, politics and mankind. Find and read the letters. Was the advice helpful? Why or why not?

Two famous advice givers today are Ann Landers and Dear Abby. Read the advice column by one of these women for several days. Find one bit of advice with which you disagree. Clip the column and **write the advice** that you would give. Tell why you disagree.

September 23

Planet Neptune Discovered 1846

Before this planet was actually seen at the Urania Observatory in Berlin, astronomers predicted its existence by using mathematics. We now know much about Neptune. Find a book about planets and prepare a **chart which compares** Neptune to Earth.

Include on your chart:

Time to orbit the sun
Time to rotate on its axis
Main gasses
Satellites

Could humans survive on Neptune?
Why or why not?

September 24

Supreme Court Founded
1789

Below are the names of several outstanding Justices of the Supreme Court. Which, in your **opinion,** was the most controversial? Give reasons for your choice.

John Jay   John Marshall   Harlan F. Stone

Earl Warren   Warren E. Burger   Thurgood Marshall

September 25

Yosemite National Park Established 1890

National parks are important to the environment as places where plant and animal wildlife are protected. 80% of the forests that existed at the beginning of our nation's history have disappeared.

Read *Going Green: A Kid's Handbook to Saving the Planet* by John Elkington or another book about protecting our natural resources.

With so many big problems facing our planet, you might not think that you can make a difference. But everything you do has an effect on the environment, even things as simple as buying a can of soda or brushing your teeth. You CAN help save the environment, and *Going Green* shows you how.

Compose a **class book "Saving the Planet from A-Z."**

For each letter of the alphabet list something you can do to improve our planet.

September 26

Birthday of John Chapman 1775-1845

Better known as Johnny Appleseed, John Chapman traveled the United States planting apple trees as he went. **Answer these questions** about him.

1. When did he begin his travels? _____
2. Through which states did he roam? _____
3. What was peculiar about him? _____
4. What is harmful to an appple tree? _____

September 27

Birthday of Thomas Nast 1840-1902

This political cartoonist is credited with creating many of the cartoon figures we are familiar with today. Which of the following are creations of Thomas Nast?

A) Democratic Donkey
B) Republican Elephant
C) Santa Claus
D) Tammany Tiger
E) Mickey Mouse
F) Sad Sack

Find a political cartoon in your daily paper. Clip and mount the cartoon. Underneath, write a **paragraph explaining** the meaning of the cartoon.

September 28

Birthday of Confucius 551 B.C. - 479 B.C.

Confucius was a Chinese philosopher whose ideas strongly influenced Chinese thought. Rewrite each of his sayings that follow using modern language and terms.

"The cautious seldom err."

"Things that are done it is needless to speak about. Things that are past it is needless to blame."

Write three modern day **proverbs** of your own to give advice to people working with computers or **using other modern inventions**.

September 29

Ladder Cimbing Record

On this date in 1997 ten Irish firemen set a record for the greatest distance climbed on a ladder in 24 hours. The team of ten climbed 102.62 kilometers using a standard fire ladder.

Compile a **Record Book** for your class. Interview each student. What can each claim that no one else in the class can claim? Records might include the largest number of siblings, the oldest grandparent, places visited or lived in, a physical accomplishment, a famous ancestor, an unusual birthday or any other claim a student can make that no other student in the class can make.

September 30

Riddle Day!

What do you call a caterpillar that was run over by a truck? *A flatterpillar*

It's easy to create an animal riddle book. Think of words that rhyme with the first few letters of the animal name. Example: *hip*popotamus: *slip, drip, flip*

Then make the riddle:

What do you call a hippopotamus acrobat? *A flippopotamus*

What do you call a rattlesnake that fights? *A battlesnake*

What do you call a wallaby that shops? *A mallaby*

How many animal riddles can you make? Write and **illustrate an animal riddle book** for others to enjoy.

October 1

The First Model T Rolls off the Assembly Line 1908

This first car cost $850.00, but as more were produced by 1924 the cost dropped to $290.00. It was lightweight, simple to operate and had a top speed of 40 miles per hour. It had good acceleration and its high clearance was perfect for the rutted, unpaved roads of the time. By 1927, there were fifteen million Model Ts on the road.

Write a dialogue between a Model T salesman and a prospective buyer. What will the salesman say? What will be some of the buyer's concerns? **Perform the dialogue** with one of your classmates.

October 2

Problem Solving Day

Almost every Mother Goose character had a problem. Miss Muffet wanted to get rid of the spider that was bothering her. Peter's wife was trapped in a rotten pumpkin shell. Humpty Dumpty couldn't be put back together again. Choose one of the **problems to solve**. Use the grid to help you. List your ideas and evaluate each one using the criteria by scoring 1 for **no**, 2 for **maybe** and 3 for **yes**. Total the scores for each idea. The idea with the highest score is the one to try.

IDEAS	FAST	SAFE	LOW COST	EFFECTIVE	TOTAL

Write and illustrate a second verse showing your solution to the problem.

October 3

Birthday of William Gorgas 1854-1920

William Gorgas helped make possible the building of the Panama Canal by destroying the mosquitoes and rats that carried disease in that area.

Complete this **math quiz.**

A. Write the year that Gorgas went to Cuba.   _____

B. How many years later did he become
   chief sanitation officer of the Panama Canal Zone?   _____

C. Multiply the number of years he spent in Panama
   by the number of years he spent in Africa.   _____

D. Add the number of years he served as Surgeon
   General of the U.S. Army.   _____

E. Total all the numbers.   _____

October 4

Citizens Band Radio Ten Four Day

Here is a letter from a trucker to his mother. **Name** all the **states** he could possibly have traveled in. Be prepared to prove your answers.

Dear Mom,

What a way to see the country! I started in California and drove the whole length of U.S. 101. Then I headed east over the Oregon trail and camped one night in a redwood stand. I backtracked southwest and crossed the Rio Grande twice and the Rocky Mountains three times. Some awesome sights I saw were the Smokies, the Dells, the White Mountains and the Northern Lights.

Looking forward to getting home and meeting you under the Arch soon.

Ten Four,
Joe

October 5

Birthday of Robert Goddard 1882-1945

Robert Goddard is called the Father of Modern Rocketry. His work led directly to the development of intercontinental missiles, earth satellites and the exploration of space.

Goddard has many "firsts" to his credit. Read about this famous scientist and **list** as many of his "firsts" as you can find. Create a **collage** of pictures from newspapers and old magazines that shows technology that would not exist if it were not for the work of Robert Goddard.

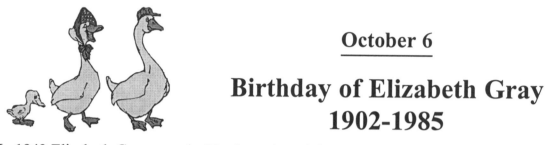

October 6

Birthday of Elizabeth Gray 1902-1985

In 1943 Elizabeth Gray won the Newbery Award for *Adam of the Road*, a tale of a young boy in another age whose travels teach him much. The book is as exciting to read today as when it was published. In the book, Adam's friend, Simon, teaches him the right words for groups of different kinds of birds. He talks about a *flight* of swallows, a *walk* of snipe and a *gaggle* of geese. Other animals also have special group names. Find and **name** as many animal groups as you can.

October 7

Birthday of Robert Westall 1929

Among the most popular books of this well-known writer is *The Devil On the Road*. In this story a young Englishman finds himself time-tripped back to 1647. As he surveys this period he realizes that he possesses much modern knowledge that could help to make the people's lives better.

If you could choose only one piece of modern knowledge to share with these people, what would it be? Write a short **essay explaining** your choice and how it would improve the quality of life in 1647. Consider:

A. It it something you are actually able to share?
B. Will it improve the lives of many people?
C. How difficult would it be to get the people to accept the new knowledge?

October 8

Barnam & Bailey's Circus Ship Returns from Europe 1902

New Yorkers who were assembled at the pier when the ship was ready to unload its animal passengers thought they were seeing a re-creation of Noah's Ark.

Research the life of a circus animal. How are they obtained? How are they cared for? What and how much do they eat? How are they trained? How often do they perform? Present your information as an **acrostic** with each sentence beginning with these letters:

```
C          A
I          N
R          I
C          M
U          A
S          L
```

October 9

Birthday of John Lennon 1940-1980

John Lennon was a member of the Beatles, a group credited with raising rock music to an art form.

Each member of the Beatles had a very different personality. Can you **match** the individual Beatle with his personality trait? What is your information source?

John Lennon	common sense
Paul McCartney	explosive
George Harrison	witty
Ringo Starr	withdrawn

Choose one of the Beatles and write a **verse** about him to sing to one of these tunes:

"Yellow Submarine"	"Help"	"Hey Jude"
"Here Comes the Sun"	"Penny Lane"	"Magical Mystery Tour"

October 10

First Synthetic Detergent 1933

Synthetic detergents clean like soap but have a completely different chemical make-up. Detergents usually work better than soap because they penetrate soiled areas better and work in all kinds of water. Environmentalists want these detergents banned because they say they are harmful to the Earth.

Read about detergents used today. How harmful are they? Write a **paragraph giving reasons** whether or not they should be banned.

October 11

Birthday of Eleanor Roosevelt 1884-1962

Read about this great woman's life in one of the many sources available. These include:

The Story of Eleanor Roosevelt by Jeanette Eaton

Eleanor Roosevelt by Jane Goodsell

Young Eleanor by Barbara Cooney

Or find articles about her on the Internet. Go to http:www.ajkids.com and enter her name in the subject box.

List and rank order five of her accomplishments from the one you think is the most important to the least important.

October 12

Columbus Discovers America 1492

If you were the captain of a small ship the size of the *Santa Maria* it would be your job to keep order and to see that each person did his job. You would need to have rules and consequences for breaking the rules.

Read about life on the *Santa Maria*. **Determine** what rules you would make as captain. What consequences would there be for breaking the rules?

Rule _____

Consequence _____

Rule _____

Consequence _____

Rule _____

Consequence _____

October 13

White House Cornerstone Laid 1792

George Washington laid the cornerstone for the White House. Find out if he was the first president to live there.

To find out what happens when a a new president moves into the White House read the fascinating book *From the Door of the White House* by Preston Bruce or use other sources to discover how many other people have jobs at the White House. List the different jobs done and give a one sentence **job description** of each.

Would you like to have one of these jobs? If so, which one? Why?

October 14

Establishment of Peace Corps 1960

This organization was established to work for peace using volunteers to raise the living standards of people in developing countries. Research and **answer these questions**.

Age to enter: If 18 and over circle **H**. If 21 and over circle **G**.
Training period: If six months circle **J**. If twelve weeks circle **E**.
Where? If in the U.S. circle **M**. If in a host country circle **L**.
Pay: If high pay circle **S**. If low pay circle **P**.

If you have circled the correct letters you will have spelled the purpose of the Peace Corps.

October 15

Hurricane Thanksgiving Day

Today is a day of thankfulness set aside by survivors of hurricanes. Use an almanac to **complete this information** about famous hurricanes of the 20th century.

NAME	DATE	WHERE HIT
A) Donna	1960	_____
B) Betsy	1965	_____
C) Beulah	1967	_____
D) Camille	1969	_____
E) Celia	1970	_____

October 16

Dictionary Day

Use your dictionary to **decode** these "incognito" book titles disguised as synonyms. Develop your own Incognito Titles for others to solve.

A. Procreated Uninhibited_____

B. The Unrelenting Stannic Combatant_____

C. The Minute Power Machine Professing Proficiency_____

D. Chartreuse Ova in Addition to Smoked Razorback_____

October 17

Black Poetry Day

Choose one of these African American poets and find several of his or her poems.

Paul Lawrence Dunbar   Langston Hughes   Countee Cullen
Gwendolyn Brooks   Nikki Giovanni

Choose a favorite poem to **illustrate** using pictures from old newspapers or magazines arranged in a **collage**. Show your illustration and read aloud the poem.
Write an original poem. Use this pattern from a poem by Langston Hughes:

Hold fast to truth, for if truth dies,
Life is a pock-filled road covered with lies.

Choose a value (love, courage, etc.)

Hold fast to _____

For if _____ _____

Life is a _____

October 18

Acronym Day

When the first letter of each word in the name of an organization spells a word, it is called an *acronym*. Witches might belong to an organization called S.P.E.L.L. (Scientifically Perfect Enchantments Lacking Love)

Decide what the letters could stand for in each of the *acronyms* below:

A) The seven dwarfs belong to the miner's union M.I.N.E.

_____

B) Casey belongs to the baseball team O.U.T.

_____

C) Railroad hero Casey Jones belongs to P.U.S.H.

_____

October 19

Sandwich Invented 1744

A) **Find** the name of the person who invented the sandwich.

_____

B) Select three current television personalities. **Decide** what might be the favorite sandwich of each and why.

1._____

_____

2._____

_____

3._____

_____

October 20

Opening of P. T. Barnum's Circus 1873

These world famous circus performers are remembered for their skill and daring. **Discover** what each did.

A) Antoinette Concello_____

B) Clyde Beatty_____

C) Mable Stark_____

D) The Wallendas_____

October 21

Birthday of Alfred Nobel 1833-1896

This Swedish chemist who invented dynamite is best remembered for the funding of the Nobel prizes for outstanding accomplishments in six areas of human endeavor. Check an almanac and **list** the winners in each area for the past year.

AREA	WINNER

October 22

Birthday of Franz Liszt 1811-1886

This gifted composer, pianist and teacher began performing professionally at the age of eleven. Read about Liszt's life. **Support or deny** each of the following sayings about gifted people as they apply to the life of Liszt. Tell whether the statement is true or not true.
A) Early giftedness wears out early.
B) Gifted people are antisocial.
C) Gifted people are concerned only about themselves and their work.

October 23

Clark Kent Proposes to Lois Lane in Superman Comic Strip 1990

The actor best known for playing the part of Superman is Christopher Reeve. He was an avid sportsman and flew his own plane across the Atlantic. In 1995 he was thrown from a horse and became paralyzed from the neck down. He is totally dependent on others for all of his needs today, yet he has become an even greater Superman by the things he has accomplished since his accident.

Read about Christopher Reeve on the Internet or other source. **List** his accomplishments since the accident. **Do you agree** that he is indeed a Superman today?
Accomplishments

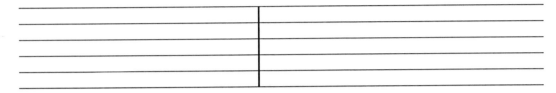

October 24

Fountain of Youth Day

In 1514 Juan Ponce de Leon discovered Florida. He was looking for the legendary Fountain of Youth. Think carefully about what would happen if you drank from a fountain and remained the age you are now forever.

List the advantages and disadvantages of never growing old.

ADVANTAGES	DISADVANTAGES

October 25

Animal Myth Day

Find out if these statements about animals are true or not true. Create a **Fact and Fiction book**. Make a statement about the animal on one page. On the next page tell your reader whether the statement is fact or fiction and why.

1. Bats are blind.
2. Owls are very wise.
3. Camels store water in their humps.
4. Squirrels can't fly.
5. Bulls attack when they see red.
6. Porcupines shoot their quills.

October 26

First Mule Imported to U.S. 1785

Research information about mules. Use the information for a **story** by choosing one item from each of the lists below. Remember, one main character must be a mule.

Character	Setting	Problem
prospector	desert	the gold was missing
farmer	city	can't find the way home
young girl	farm	must get crops in before the storm comes
actor/actress	train	train held up by bandits
doctor	wilderness	must reach sick child before dark

October 27

Colombia Volcano Erupts Overnight Killing 20,000 1985

There are three types of volcanoes: active, dormant and extinct. In the United States, Mt. St. Helens is an active volcano as are many volcanoes in Hawaii.

Illustrate a chart that explains the difference between the three types of volcanoes. Give the name and location of at least two of each kind.

October 28

Statue of Liberty Dedicated 1886

Immigrants who arrived in New York Harbor after this date have been greeted by the sight of the Statue of Liberty. Use the encyclopedia or other reference sources to **answer these questions.**

1. Who was the sculptor who created the Statue?_____
2. What was his nationality?_____
3. What part of the structure were Americans responsible for raising the money to build?
_____
4. Who was president when the Statue of Liberty was dedicated?
_____
5. Who wrote *"Give me your tired, your poor, your huddled masses yearning to be free."*
_____
6. What symbol of illumination does the Statue hold?_____
7. What metal is used as the skin of the statue?_____
8. Why do you think the Statue is important?
_____

October 29

National Organization of Women Formed 1966

This organization promotes equal rights for women. Here are some good books with female heroines. Read one of the books and post an **illustrated review** in your classroom or library.

The Drakenberg Adventure by Lloyd Alexander   *Caddie Woodlawn* by Carol Ryrie Brink
The Philadelphia Adventure by Lloyd Alexander *Dicey's Song* by Cynthia Voigt
The Great Gilly Hopkins by Betsy Byars   *A Wrinkle in Time* by Madeleine L' Engle

October 30

Ball Point Pen Patented 1888

This invention made it possible for people to carry pens with them without taking along a bottle of ink.

Think of something that is troublesome to do that you do quite frequently.

_____

What **invention** is needed to simplify the task?

_____

_____

Combine at least four of these items so that one acts on the next one to create the invention.

A 20 pound weight	a candle	a long rope	a bucket	a bottle
a match	a broom	four nails	a blanket	a cup
ice cubes	a wagon	a car tire	a chain	a hammer
an umbrella	a balloon			

Draw a picture of your invention and **write a description** of how it works.

October 31

Halloween

What a great day to read a ghost story! **Read** one of these and create a **poster** to sell the book to others.

The Ghost Belonged to Me by Richard Peck
   The ghost will continue haunting Alexander's barn until he returns its bones to their proper resting place.

Ghost Children by Eve Bunting
   Matt investigates the vandalism of life-sized dolls belonging to his strange aunt.

Ghost Followed Us Home by Peg Kehret
   Two girls are trapped in a museum with a ghost.

Who Knew There'd Be Ghosts? by Bill Brittain
   Three children and a trio of ghosts outwit a stranger's plan to turn the old Parnell House into a museum.

Ghost in the Big Brass Bed by Bruce Coville
   Two young girls investigate the appearance of a little girl ghost.

Ghost in the House by Daniel Cohen
   Real life tales of haunted houses.

November 1

Authors' Day

Celebrate this day by developing a **list** of five guidelines for identifying great authors. Take a **poll**. Ask classmates to nominate an author who meets the guidelines. Post the list of authors nominated.

Hold an election (classmates who nominated an author can campaign for their choices). Collect as much information as you can about the winning author and his or her books and prepare a **bulletin board** display.

November 2

Birthday of Daniel Boone 1734-1820

This famous pioneer/explorer was described as generous, humane, knowledgeable and a natural leader. Explore his life by **writing questions** to the answers below.

A) The answer is *Wilderness Trail*. What is the question?

_____

B) The answer is the *Shawnee Indians*. What is the question?

_____

C) The answer is *Rebecca*. What is the question?

_____

D) The answer is *Boonesborough*. What is the question?

_____

November 3

Japan Culture Day

Find and **read** one of the following books. **Review the book** for your class. Note especially how the customs of the Japanese people are shown.

Crow Boy by Taro Yashima
The Big Wave by Pearl Buck
The Crane Maiden by Mijoko Matsutani
Hiroshima No Pika by Toshi Maruki

The Wave by Margaret Hodges
The Golden Crane by Yamaguchi
The Mud Snail Son by Betty Lifton

November 4

Discovery of the Tomb of Tutankahmen 1933

This discovery by Howard Carter revealed the tomb of a young king who died in the year 1335 B.C. A mystery surrounds his death. **Read** *The Awful Egyptians* by Terry Deary or another book about King Tut. What do you think? Was he murdered? If so, who did it? Who did Tut's wife marry after his death? What relationship was she to her second husband?

Write a paper that **answers these questions**.

November 5

First Automobile Patent Issued 1895

Find out what it costs to own a car today. **Survey** car owners to find the following costs. Assume that you want to purchase a new car.

Make/Model of the car   _____

Initial cost   _____

Interest charges   _____

Sales Tax   _____

Insurance for one year   _____

Personal property tax for one year_____

License   _____

Inspection charge   _____

Gas for 10,000 miles   _____

Annual tune up   _____

Two oil changes   _____

Depreciation   _____

Total for one year   _____

November 6

Book Report Day

In astrology it is held that one's birthdate and the sign of the Zodiac under which one is born will determine basic personality characteristics. Here are some of the characteristics a person might be expected to have if born under the following signs:

Aries:	Natural leader, competitive, forceful
Leo:	Perceptive about people, tolerant, trusting
Sagittarius:	Active and athletic, restless
Taurus:	Loyal, devoted, hardworking
Virgo:	Gentle, independent, calm, likes details
Capricorn:	Cautious, good organizer, urge to succeed
Gemini:	Charming, life of the party
Libra:	Honest, able to see both sides of a problem
Aquarius:	Relentless, untiring worker, seeker of truth
Cancer:	Modest, thrifty, likes comfort
Scorpio:	Good sense of money, realistic, resourceful
Pisces:	Creative, imaginative, great love for others

Name three book characters that you believe might have been born under any of the signs above. **Cite 1 incident** from the book to show why you chose a certain sign for the character.

November 7

Birthday of James Naismith, Inventor of Basketball

Read *Encyclopedia Brown's Book of Wacky Sports* by Donald Sobol. **Answer these questions**.

1. What was the secret weapon of the 1978 Chinese National Basketball Team?

_____

2. What college basketball team lost 99 consecutive games?

_____

3. What NBA star changed his name?

_____

4. What player scored 97 points in one basketball game?

_____

5. What was the wettest day for basketball in the history of Florida?

_____

November 8

Aid and Abet Punsters' Day

Puns are plays on words. Authors who use many puns in their books are Roy Doty (*Pinocchio Was Nosey*) and Larry Shles (*Nose Drops*).

Have fun with nose puns or owl puns. **Illustrate** and label pun trading cards. Examples: An owl in a blender would be "Owl Mixed Up." A magazine about noses might be titled *Snorts Illustrated.*

November 9

Birthday of Elijah Lovejoy 1802-1837

Lovejoy was a minister and an editor who expressed his views about anti-slavery in the *St. Louis Observer*. His unpopular views caused him to leave St. Louis and set up his presses in Alton, Illinois. Two presses were destroyed but still he continued to publish.

Read about his life in the encyclopedia or on the Internet. **Answer these questions.**

1. What happened to Lovejoy as he continued to defend the freedom of the press?
_____
_____

2. Name two other dissenters who paid the same price for defending their views.
_____
_____

November 10

Sinking of the *Edmund Fitzgerald* 1975

The *Edmund Fitzgerald* was an ore barge sunk in Lake Superior in 25 foot waves. All aboard were lost. The difficult oil slick clean-up was a cooperative effort of the United States and Canada. A more recent oil slick disaster occurred off the shores of Alaska.

Read about and **list** five dangers of oil slicks. **Rank order** your list from the greatest to the least danger.

1_____
2._____
3._____
4._____
5._____

November 11

End of World War I 1918

Encyclopedia **Quick Quiz**
1. Who fired the two shots that started the war?

_____

2. Who were the five principal allies?

_____

3. What was the length of the war?

_____

4. Who were the Central Powers?

_____

5. Who was President of the United States during the war?

_____

November 12

First Man on the Flying Trapeze: Jules Leotard 1859

Jules Leotard was a famous French aerialist credited with the invention of leotards in 1859. Many items we use get their names from famous people. **List** for whom the following were named.

1. Saxophone_____
2. Levis_____
3. Dukes_____
4. Boycott_____

November 13

Invention of Peanut Butter 1890

The peanut is one of the most useful of plants. Since the pods develop underground, peanuts are often called ground nuts. George Washington Carver is credited with finding over 300 uses for the peanut. **Research** the peanut and **list** eight important uses.

1._____   2._____
3._____   4._____
5._____   6._____
7._____   8._____

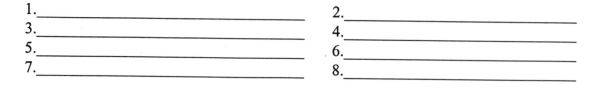

November 14

Birthday of Claude Monet 1840-1926

Monet was one of the first artists of his day to paint impressions of scenes rather than produce exact detail. **Locate** a reproduction of one of Monet's paintings. List the title here:

_____

List ten words that come to mind as your first impression of the painting. Combine the words along with any other words needed to write a **poem describing** the painting. Your poem does not have to rhyme.

November 15

Founding of the American Federation of Labor 1881

Create your own important organization by selecting one word from each list below. Write a **paragraph explaining** who your organization serves, why it is important and what it does for its members.

Agency	For	Urban	Resources
Bureau	Regarding	Retail	Rights
Organization	Mandating	Civil	Neglect
Committee	Concerning	Foreign	Expenditure
Workers	Eliminating	Criminal	Production

November 16

Birthday of Jean Fritz 1915

Born in China of American parents, Jean Fritz is one of the best known children's authors of historical fiction.

Complete these titles of five of her books.

1. *And Then What Happened* _____?
2. *Why Don't You Get A* _____, *Sam Adams?*
3. *Where Was* _____ *on the 29th of May?*
4. *What's the* _____ , *Ben Franklin?*
5. *Will You Sign Here,* _____?

Choose one of the books and create an **advertisement** for it. Post it on the class bulletin board.

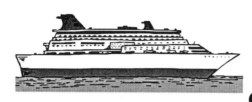

November 17

Opening of the Suez Canal 1869

Research the answers to this Suez **Math Quiz**.

A. Length of the Canal   _____

B. Number of seas it joins   _____

C. Shortened the route between
   England and India by   _____

D. Depth   _____

E. Width at bottom   _____

F. Width at surface   _____

G. Number of letters in the last
   name of the builder   _____

H. Year construction began   _____

I. Year the canal opened   _____

Total of all numbers   _____

If all of your answers are correct your total should be 10,393.

November 18

Feat of William Tell 1307

The legend is told of this Swiss hero that he defied the ruler of the land by refusing to take his hat off as the ruler passed by. His punishment was to shoot an apple off his son's head with an arrow. **Read** an encyclopedia article or one of the many illustrated tales about William Tell. Complete this sentence giving **evidence for your conclusions**.

I believe William Tell *was or was not* a real person because_____

_____

_____

_____

_____

_____

November 19

Birthday of George Rogers Clark 1752-1818

This famous explorer has many firsts to his credit. **List** at least three.

_____

_____

_____

In reading about George Rogers Clark in different reference books, **compare** all the accounts of his life. Did they agree? If not, what was one area of disagreement?

_____

_____

Check the facts in a third reference book. Which do you think is correct?

November 20

DDT Use Halted in Residential Areas

Use an encyclopedia or the Internet to **discover** what DDT is and the dangers in using it.

DDT is

_____

It is used for

_____

Dangers in using DDT are

_____

_____

_____

_____

November 21

World Hello Day

Create a **drawing** or a **collage** from magazine pictures of people and customs of other lands. Below the collage list the countries represented. After each country write the word "*HELLO*" in the language of that country.

The 400 section of the library will have books written in many languages.

November 22

Assassination of John F. Kennedy 1963

John F. Kennedy, former President of the United States, was killed by an assassin's bullet while riding in a motorcade in Dallas, Texas. Use *Bartlett's Quotations* to determine who said each of the quotes below. Which was said by John F. Kennedy? Write a short **paragraph** telling what you think he meant by these words.

1. *"Dare to be true. Nothing needs a lie."*_____

2. *"They can conquer who believe they can."*_____

3. *"Ask not what your country can do for you. Ask what you can do for your country."*

   _____

4. *"A penny saved is a penny earned."*_____

5. *"The only thing we have to fear is fear itself."*_____

November 23

Birthday of William H. Bonney (Billy the Kid) 1859-1881

Billy the Kid was an outlaw in the Wild West who boasted of killing twenty-one men. Here is a tough **Wild West quiz**. How many answers can you find?

1. Who cleaned up crime in Abilene, Texas?_____

2. Who was appointed U.S. Marshall in 1905 by President Teddy Roosevelt?

   _____

3. Who killed Billy the Kid?_____

4. Who established one of the first detective agencies in the United States?

   _____

5. Who was the judge known as *"The Law West of the Pecos?"* _____

6. In what state was the OK Corral?_____

November 24

Birthday of Father Serra 1713-1784

Despite his lameness, Father Serra traveled extensively throughout the Southwest and established many missions including the first mission in California. Find books about explorers of the West and Southwest for information about Father Serra and his travels.

Draw a **map** showing Father Serra's travels. Use appropriate symbols on your map to show the different problems he encountered on his travels.

November 25

Birthday of Joe Dimaggio 1915-1999

In 1941 this famous baseball player set a Major League record hitting safely in fifty-six consecutive games. He is considered one of the all time greats of baseball.

Check an almanac or one of the many baseball encyclopedias to **find** the accomplishments of current baseball stars. Which of the current players would you nominate for the Baseball Hall of Fame? Why?

PLAYER	ACCOMPLISHMENT
_____	_____
_____	_____
_____	_____
_____	_____

November 26

Birthday of Charles Schulz 1922-2000

Charles Schulz was the creator of the *Peanuts* comic strip which features Charlie Brown, Lucy, Linus, Snoopy and friends. In the strip Charlie Brown often has problems being accepted by his friends.

Look in the telephone book. Find and **list** two products or services Charlie Brown could use to gain popularity.

1._____

Used to_____

2._____

Used to_____

November 27

Birthday of Robert Livingstone 1746-1813

This American statesman who helped write the Declaration of Independence does not receive nearly as much attention in history books as his accomplishments deserve. **Read** about his life and **identify** those accomplishments below which should be credited to him.

_____ Administered the Oath of Office to George Washington

_____ Served as a delegate to the Continental Congress

_____ Served as a judge on the New York Court of Chancery

_____ Negotiated the Louisiana Purchase with France

_____ Helped Robert Fulton build the steamboat *Clermont*

November 28

First Automobile Race in America 1895

The *Guinness Book of World Records* has many interesting facts about automobiles and auto racing. It describes the longest, fastest, greatest speed, distance and other facts. Read through the records listed about automobiles and **list** the records that amaze you the most.

1._____
_____
_____

2._____
_____
_____

3._____
_____
_____

4._____
_____
_____

Create an **Automobile Record Book** using these and other facts. **Illustrate** the book.

November 29

Richard Byrd Flies Over the South Pole 1929

Byrd made three flights over the South Pole between 1929 and 1957. He led numerous expeditions to the bleak, frozen continent of Antarctica. Each expedition undertook numerous scientific experiments.

Read one of the following books or another book about the exploration of Antarctica.

The Conquest of the North and South Poles by Russell Owen

Antarctic: Bottom of the World by Julian May

How Did We Find Out About Antarctica? by Isaac Asimov

Pretend you are a member of one of the expeditions. **Write a letter** home telling of your experiences. Include in your letter a **description** of one of the scientific experiments your team is conducting.

November 30

Save the Rain Forest Day

Tropical rain forests cover about six percent of the Earth's surface yet one half of all living species on this planet live in the rain forests. Unfortunately, more than twenty-five million acres of trees in the rain forests are cut each year. Much of the oxygen needed to sustain all life comes from the rain forests. They are sometimes called "The lungs of the Earth."

Read about the rain forests in the encyclopedia or on the Internet. **Answer these questions.**

1. How many kinds of trees can you name?

2. Name all the ways that trees can be destroyed.

3. How many uses can you name for trees that are left to live in the rain forest, park or your yard?

4. How many products can you name that are made from trees?

5. What might we use instead of trees to make these products?

6. What can you do to help save our trees?

December 1

Rosa Parks Day 1955

The Montgomery, Alabama, bus boycott was a direct result of the courage of one woman, Rosa Parks, who refused to give up her seat on a segregated bus. The success of the boycott convinced many that civil rights could be achieved by direct action. The women listed below have played important roles in our country's history. Discover which of these women, like Rosa Parks, worked to extend civil rights to all. Write an **interview** as if you were the reporter asking her **questions** and giving what you believe her **answers** would be.

Margaret Corbin	Clara Barton	Lucretia Mott
Angelina Grimke	Ruth Benedict	Elizabeth Dole
Mary Terrell	Sandra Day O'Connor	Eleanor Roosevelt

December 2

Birthday of George Seurat 1859-1891

When this famous painter died at the age of 32 most of his paintings were unsold. One reason for this was that he founded an entirely new style of painting called *pointillism*. Find reproductions of two paintings by Seurat. **Read** about pointillism and **tell** what it is.

Find a poem that you believe goes with each painting. Show the paintings and read aloud the poems. Explain to your class what pointillism is.

December 3

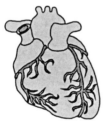

First Heart Transplant 1967

The first heart transplant was performed by Dr. Christian Bernard of South Africa. Read about the well-known causes of heart disease. Which two forms of heart disease can be prevented? _____

_____

List five things a person can do who wants to maintain a strong, healthy heart.

1. _____
2. _____
3. _____
4. _____
5. _____

Create a **poster** that shows what one must do to have a healthy heart.

December 4

Phonograph Produced 1877

When Thomas Edison invented the phonograph, little did he know the number of jobs he would create. Read about the recording industry. **List** six jobs that would not exist today if not for Edison's invention.

_____   _____   _____
_____   _____   _____

Name another recent invention. _____ List new jobs that were created because of it.

_____   _____   _____
_____   _____   _____

December 5

Birthday of George A. Custer 1839-1876

On June 25, 1876, Custer led 225 of his men into the Battle of Little Bighorn. None survived and controversy about the battle still exists today. Did Custer, as some say, disobey orders and lead his men into battle seeking glory for himself? Or did Custer, with full authority, lead the charge in the belief that other columns led by Major Reno would join the battle?

Read two accounts of Custer's Last Stand. Write a **paragraph** telling what you believe the truth to be.

December 6

Birthday of Cornelia Meigs 1884-1973

Cornelia Meigs is the author of the Newbery Award biography of Louisa May Alcott. In *Invincible Louisa* the author tells how Louisa May Alcott had faith in herself even though others believed she could not write.

Here are other famous people who did not do well in school. **List** what each is remembered for.

1. Jack London   _____

2. Thomas A. Edison   _____

3. Winston Churchill   _____

4. Roald Dahl   _____

5. Henry Ford   _____

December 7

Japanese Attack Pearl Harbor 1941

At 7:55 a.m. on this day the American Pacific Fleet was attacked at Pearl Harbor by Japan. Two hours later the United States had lost eighteen ships including eight battleships and 170 planes. This was the beginning of four years of war in the Pacific.

Check the library card catalog to find the authors of these titles. Each tells what happened to loyal Japanese American citizens during World War II. **Review the book** you choose for your class.

Journey to Topaz by _____

Farewell to Manzanar by _____

December 8

First Christmas Card Produced 1843

This first card was produced by a printing company in London and started the use of printed rather than hand-written holiday messages in both England and the United States. **Evaluate** the sending of printed rather than hand-written holiday greetings.

ADVANTAGES	DISADVANTAGES

December 9

Birthday of Joel Chandler Harris 1848-1908

This journalist became famous for his *Uncle Remus* stories which were considered to be a valuable addition to American folklore. The folk hero of these stories was Brer Rabbit.

Below are the initials of other American folk heroes. Can you give their **names**?

J.M. _____   J.H._____

P.B._____   P.B._____

F.F._____   D.C._____

December 10

Birthday of Melvil Dewey 1851-1931

Melvil Dewey devised a system for organizing library books so that books on the same subject are found together. He did this by giving each category of knowledge a different number. To discover how this system works, take a trip around the library to see what subjects are represented by the numbers given below. **Fill in each blank** with the subject.

WHAT A TRIP!

_____700 decided to travel by_____629.13 to_____917.47. He knew he would get to cross some famous _____624.2 as he traveled in the area. He had read about the city in his _____027.8. He wanted to experience the_____535 the _____535.6 and _____534 of a big city. He went to the zoo to see _____591, _____597, _____598.1 and _____598.2. He also wanted to go to a _____796.33 game while he was there.

The _____303.34 was a lot different from his own home. These people had no room for a _____635 or to raise _____636.1 or _____636.5 the way his family did. The _____720 was different from what he was used to at home in _____917.72

_____700 attended a _____792 while he was in the city. He saw a _____793.8 show, too. On his next trip he would like to take a _____387.2 to _____919.69.

December 11

Abdication of Edward VIII 1936

Edward the VIII of Great Britain is best remembered because he gave up his throne for what he considered to be a very important reason. **Answer these questions**.

1. What was the reason?_____

2. Who became the new king?_____

3. What relationship is Queen Elizabeth II to Edward VIII? _____

4. How powerful is the ruler of Great Britain today? _____

Defend your answer.

December 12

Poinsettia Day

If the discoverer of this plant:

Was a woman, circle T. If a man, circle J.	T J
Was a southerner, circle O. If a northerner, circle Y	O Y
Was President of the U.S., circle N. If Secretary of War, circle E.	E N
If the poinsettia is a flower, circle S. If not a flower, circle L.	S L

The answers to the quiz spell the first name of the person who discovered this plant.

This plant was discovered by _____Poinsett.

December 13

Sir Francis Drake Sets Sail Around the World 1577

Read about this trip including the places visited, the route followed and the conditions aboard ship. As Captain, Sir Francis Drake surely had to make rules to be followed on the ship. If you were the Captain of this voyage **list** five rules you consider to be essential. **Rank order** your rules in order of importance.

Illustrate your rules on a **poster**.

December 14

Discovery of the South Pole 1911

Complete this article.

SOUTH POLE DISCOVERED

Explorer _____ _____ arrived at the South Pole, the point where all the Earth's lines of _____ meet, on December 13, 1911. He beat _____ _____ of England to the Pole by one month. In 1956, the U.S. established a permanent scientific base at the pole and in honor of both early explorers it was named The _____ _____ South Pole Station.

December 15

Bill of Rights Day

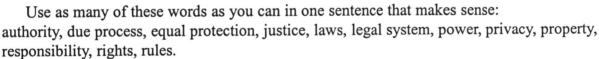

What are the four major freedoms guaranteed by the Bill of Rights?

_____   _____

_____   _____

Use as many of these words as you can in one sentence that makes sense: authority, due process, equal protection, justice, laws, legal system, power, privacy, property, responsibility, rights, rules.

December 16

Birthday of Ludwig Van Beethoven 1770-1827

Compare these three great composers on this chart.

Factors in Life	Beethoven	Handel	Mozart
Composed at an early age			
Helped by parents			
Handicapped			
Died before age 50			

From the chart can you draw any **conclusions** about common factors in the life of a composer? Research the lives of more composers to see if your conclusions hold up.

December 17

Wright Brothers Flight 1903

This power-driven heavier-than-air flight took place in Kitty Hawk, North Carolina. The plane was in the air 12 seconds and flew 120 feet.

Use an almanac to **discover** these other world record-setting flights.

A. Greatest speed over a straight course._____

B. Greatest speed over a closed circuit._____

C. Greatest distance in a straight line._____

D. Greatest distance over a closed circuit._____

E. Highest altitude._____

December 18

Death of Antonio Stradivarii 1644-1737

Stradivarii was one of the greatest violin makers of all time. His instruments were brilliant in tone and power and exact in every detail. Only a few of these violins remain today.

A) What would a genuine Stradivarii violin cost today?_____

B) If one suddenly came on the market, which of these musicians would play it in his next concert?

Itzhak Perlman	Carlos Montoya
Van Cliburn	Leonard Slatkin
James Galway	Andre Previn

C) Which of those listed above might conduct a concert that included a violin concerto?

_____

December 19

Coal Mine Explosion 1907

This disaster occurred in Jacobs Creek, Pennsylvania, and cost the lives of 239 miners. A 1984 pre-Christmas coal mine fire in Utah cost the lives of 27 miners. Coal is rarely used today as a home heating energy source.

1. Find out what kind of energy sources are used in your community. **List** four.
A. _____ C. _____
B. _____ D. _____

2. Of the sources you listed, which is the most efficient?
_____

Read a recent book or article about energy sources. What does the author predict will be the major energy source of the future?
_____

December 20

Hanukkah (Movable date)

FACTS FROM THE ALMANAC

1. Another name for Hanukkah:_____
2. When did this holiday begin?_____
3. Who started this holiday?_____
4. How long does the holiday last?_____
5. Who celebrates the holiday?_____
6. What is done on each day of the festival?_____

December 21

Create A Lune Day

A *lune* is a three line poem that can be used to describe a person, place or object. The first line is three words. The second line is five words and the third line is three words. Here is an example:

Can you see
Colonel Sanders eating a hamburger
At Burger King?

Write and **illustrate** three **lunes** about three different famous people.

December 22

Death of John Newbery 1767

John Newbery was an English printer and one of the first to print children's books. An annual award is given in this man's name every year by the American Library Association for the best written children's book by an American author.

Use the card catalog to find the author of these popular Newbery winners. Read and **review** one of the books for your class.

1. *Dicey's Song*
2. *Bridge to Terabithia*
3. *Westing Game*
4. *Jacob Have I Loved*
5. *Roll of Thunder, Hear My Cry*
6. *Holes*
7. *The Whipping Boy*
8. *The Midwife's Apprentice*

December 23

Create A Recipe Biography

Choose a famous person you admire. Read about that person's life. **Write and illustrate a recipe** using the main facts about the person. For example:

A RECIPE FOR SALLY RIDE
1 cup talented athlete
2 tablespoons physics and English degrees
1/2 cup astrophysics Ph.D.
1 slice astronaut application
2 large packages NASA

Mix space shuttle with
1 female flight engineer
Cook for six days, testing robot arms frequently
Remove vehicle from atmosphere
Preserve Sally Ride as the first American
woman in space

A Recipe for_____

December 24   December 25

Christmas Eve and Christmas Day

One musical event often performed during the Christmas holidays is the tale of the *Nutcracker* which was written by E. A. Hoffman in 1816. The tale has fascinated artists, composers and audiences for almost 200 years. It has retained its freshness because it appeals to the sense of wonder that we all share.

Maurice Sendak designed brilliant sets and costumes for the Pacific Northwest Ballet's Christmas production of the *Nutcracker* and has created even more beautiful illustrations for his picture book of the same title.

This magical tale combined with Tchaikovsky's music is a holiday treat for every member of the family.

Follow the newspaper listings for the month of December and **list** those theatrical and musical events that will take place in your community or a nearby city. Put a star by those works that are more than fifty years old.

1._____

2._____

3._____

4._____

5._____

6._____

7._____

8._____

9._____

10._____

Choose one of the starred listings above. **Analyze** why it is still popular today, so many years after its first performance.

_____

_____

December 26

Boxing Day

This English legal holiday began with the custom of giving Christmas boxes to tradesmen, servants and others who provide services throughout the year.

Make a **list** of five people whose services YOU depend on throughout the year. What would be an appropriate gift for each?

                                                       Gift

1. _____   _____
2. _____   _____
3. _____   _____
4. _____   _____
5. _____   _____

December 27

Birthday of Ingri d'Aulaire

This famous author is best known for the trolls she created with her husband Edgar. Here are other mythical creatures each of which is a composite of two animals. Can you **match** them? **Illustrate** your interpretation of one of them.

A. Centaur	_____	1.	man plus lion
B. Manticore	_____	2.	eagle plus dragon
C. Griffin	_____	3.	horse plus man
D. Minotaur	_____	4.	lion plus eagle
E. Basilisk	_____	5.	man plus bull

December 28

Anniversary of Poor Richard's Almanack 1733

Published by Benjamin Franklin, this almanack is best known for the many wise sayings included. Use your dictionary to **"translate"** these well-known sayings.

1. Self sustaining individuals garner almighty assistance.

_____

2. 1/100 of a preserved greenback is tantamount to a similar portion for services rendered.

_____

Try using **synonyms** for words in other Poor Richard sayings for others to "translate."

December 29

Wild Animal Day

A resume tells the most important facts about a person. Choose a wild animal. Research facts about the animal and include them in a resume. **Illustrate your resume** and post for others to enjoy. Example:

NAME:	African Lion
HEIGHT:	Five to eight feet
WEIGHT:	350-550 lbs.
DIET:	Giraffe, warthog, occasional baby elephant for dessert
HOBBIES:	Practicing great leaps and loud roars
DISPOSITION:	Generally peaceful unless hungry or challenged
ACCOMPLISHMENTS:	Star of MGM motion pictures

December 30

Help A Prince Day

Cinderella's Prince Charming had one glass slipper but no princess to wear it. Perhaps if the Prince had been a reader he might have consulted one of the famous detectives found in literature.

Name two famous detectives found in books.

_____   _____

Compose a **telegram** from the prince to one of these detectives. What will the prince want the detective to do? Remember, you must give the whole message in ten words.

December 31

Take A Letter Day

1. Name one admirable character found in literature.

_____

2. Name a character you least like from literature.

_____

Write a **letter** from the first character you named to the second giving advice about how to live a better life. Your letter should reveal facts about both characters.

January 1

New Years Day

Each New Year brings a variety of scientific and unscientific predictions. Scientific predictions are done by people called *demographers* and they are usually good predictors of the future based on what they know about population trends.

Demographers have made the following predictions about these changes in the lives of U.S. citizens by the year 2010.

Choose two of the changes and **explain** the effects on the daily lives of most people if the prediction is correct.

1. Senior citizens will double their numbers.
2. Hispanics will be the largest minority group in the United States.
3. Fewer workers will be available to pay for retirees.
4. Eighty million home computers will be in use.
5. There will be a continued increase in the number of independent voters.

January 2

The Birthday of Crosby Bonsall

Crosby Bonsall was the author of many mystery stories for both younger and older readers. Among her books are *The Case of the Cat's Meow* and *The Case of the Hungry Stranger*. From the lists that follow choose one character, one setting, one problem and one clue and **write a short mystery**.

Character	Setting	Problem
Zip, a smart dog	An old garden	The diamond ring was missing
Marie, a 10 year-old	A department store	Birds are dying
Super Brain	A mansion	A rich woman disappears
Chump, a monkey	The mall	Someone is changing the price tags

Clues		
A dead bird	A lipstick	Wet fur
A letter	A broken mirror	DDT
A key	A cellar door	A pink ribbon

January 3

Birthday of J. R. R. Tolkien 1892-1973

Many have said that the *Star Wars* movies are modern versions of Tolkein's fantasy tales. View the first *Star Wars* movie. The film can be borrowed at no charge from many public libraries. Prepare a **chart** that matches the characters in *Star Wars* to the characters in Tolkein's *The Hobbit*.

Star Wars **Character**	the same as	*Hobbit* **Character**
1. Luke Skywalker		_____
2. Ben Kenobi		_____
3. Princess Leia		_____
4. Darth Vader		_____
5. Chewbacca		_____
6. Hans Solo		_____

January 4

Birthday of Jacob Grimm 1785-1863

Jacob Grimm and his brother Wilhelm were German printers who gathered together and printed well-known fairy tales. Until the Grimm Brothers put the tales in print, the only way they could be enjoyed was by listening to storytellers.

A *simile* points out how two objects are alike using the words *like* or *as*. Here are four examples of similes found in Grimms Fairy Tales. Draw a line from each simile to the tale in which you think it would be found. Give a short **explanation** of why you made each match.

1. The Bremen Town Musicians	A. beds...all made up with coverlets as white as plum blossoms
2. Snow White & the Seven Dwarfs	B. setting in the road, looking as dismal as three wet days
3. Fisherman & His Wife	C. Her face looked like an old shriveled pear
4. Hansel and Gretel	D. The water churned as if it were boiling

Select a favorite fairy tale character and write a **one paragraph description** of the character. Include at least two similes in your description.

January 5

Death of George Washington Carver 1864-1943

This world-famous scientist developed over 300 products from the peanut, 118 products from the sweet potato and 75 products from the pecan. Scientists today continue Carver's work trying to cope with the problem of world hunger.

Find out what foods on your dinner table contain these soybean products:
1. tofu _____
2. miso _____
3. tempeh _____

January 6

Four Freedoms Speech 1941

On this day in 1941, President Franklin D. Roosevelt spoke to Congress about the four basic freedoms the United States should seek to promote everywhere in the world. These were:
1. Freedom of speech and expression
2. Freedom of worship, each in his own way
3. Freedom from want, a healthy, peaceful life for all
4. Freedom from fear with world-wide reduction of armaments

Take a **poll**. List these four freedoms and poll your classmates. Which of the four does each person polled believe is the most important. Report your results to the class.

January 7

United Nations World Literacy Day

At one time most American pioneers could not read or write. Consider how they managed to settle this country without these skills. Today's pioneers are those who are exploring space. If the early pioneers could manage to tame the wilderness and build this country without being able to read or write, do you think the space pioneers can make discoveries without these skills? Why or why not?

Brainstorm all of the disadvantages of not being able to read or write. Share your **list** with the class. Can class members name others you did not name? Make a **poster** for the bulletin board that includes your best ideas.

January 8

Birthday of Elvis Presley 1935-1977

Elvis Presley was one of the most popular rock singers of all time. With thousands of young singers trying to make it to the top of the music world, why do you believe Presley achieved such fame?

Find a book about the singer's life and complete the **puzzle**. **Add** 5 more words horizontally.

```
              P e r s o n a l i t y
              R
              E
    N e w S t y l e
              L
              E
              Y
```

January 9

First Successful Balloon Flight by Jean Pierre Blanchard 1793

An exciting book about a wild balloon flight is *The Twenty One Balloons* by William Pené Dubois. If you were a member of the crew on this voyage you would be forced to land on the Island of Krakatoa. The people of the island want to keep their island home a secret and so refuse to let you leave. You are supplied with every comfort and courtesy but you are carefully guarded to prevent your escape.

Decide: Do you want to escape? **List** reasons for and against.

For	Against

January 10

League of Nations Established 1920

This first attempt to bring nations of the world together later resulted in the formation of the United Nations.

One exciting way to learn more and to gain a greater understanding of nations of the world is to begin international **stamp collecting**. For a free booklet on international stamps **write a letter** requesting the *Introductory Guide to United Nations Stamps* from:

U. N. Postal Administration
P. O. Box 5900
Grand Central Station
New York, New York 10017

January 11

Birthday of Robert C. O Brien 1918-1973

In this author's award winning book, *Mrs. Frisby and the Rats of NIMH*, the rats came from NIMH. These letters stand for a special agency, the National Institute of Mental Health, which was formed in 1967 and is located in Washington, D.C. This organization conducts medical research and builds community health centers around the country for programs about drug abuse and alcoholism and improved mental health.

Use an almanac to find out what these **acronyms** stand for:

1. NAAFA	4. JA
2. ASPCA	5. DAR
3. CARE	6. AFL-CIO

January 12

Birthday of Charles Perrault 1628-1703

Charles Perrault was one of the first collectors of fairy tales including *Cinderella and the Glass Slipper*. Today there are over 400 different Cinderella tales coming from many countries and cultures of the world. Find one of these tales from another country. Good choices would be *The Egyptian Cinderella* or *The Korean Cinderella* both by Shirley Climo.

Develop a **compare/contrast chart** to show how one of these tales is both like and unlike Perrault's Cinderella.

Compare characters, setting, plot, the lost item, food, dress, transportation, animals and any other aspects of the culture that you find. Share your chart with your class.

January 13

Stephen Foster Memorial Day 1826-1864

Stephen Foster had very little musical training yet taught himself to play the clarinet at age six and could play any tune after hearing it. He became one of America's best loved composers. **Complete the titles** of these Stephen Foster songs. A good reference source would be an American songbook found in the 700s in your library.

A) ____ _____ River

B) My Old _____ Home

C) _____ Races

D) Oh! _____

Find a recording of Foster melodies in your school media center or on the Internet and listen to them. Write a **critique** telling why they are not played often today.

January 14

Birthday of Hugh Lofting 1886-1947

Hugh Lofting is best known for his book *Dr. Dolittle* about the doctor who talks to animals. In this book he creates a number of very strange animals. The pushme-pullys were rare animals with no tail and two heads. The two heads enabled them to eat and talk at the same time without being rude.

Design a rare animal. Give it an unusual feature which enables it to do something special. Draw a picture of your animal, name it and give a brief **description** of its unusual abilities.

January 15

Birthday of Martin Luther King, Jr.
1929-1968

This great leader preached civil rights through non-violent means. However, he himself became the victim of much violence. He was stabbed in New York City. He was stoned in Chicago. His Alabama home was bombed. He was killed by an assassin's bullet.

Find and read his famous "I Have A Dream" speech. List the major dreams that he had (things he wanted to see happen). Have any of the "dreams" come true since the speech was given? Which "dreams" remain to be realized?

Choose one of the "dreams" mentioned in the speech and **develop a plan** that you and your classmates can carry out to make the dream come true in your classroom.

Include in your plan:
  A. What you want to achieve
  B. Resources needed
  C. Steps to achieve the goal
  D. Obstacles to be overcome and possible solutions
  E. A time line of activities necessary to achieve the goal

January 16

National Nothing Day

Here is a day set aside to do nothing! It would be more fun, however, to read a "Nothing" book. Try one of these:

Nothing's Fair in the Fifth Grade by Barthe DeClements
Tales of a Fourth Grade Nothing by Judy Blume
Nothing's Impossible by Jeff Sheridan

Use the title of the book you read to write an **acrostic poem** about the book.

How many ways can you complete this poem:

Nothing day means that there's nothing to do.
Nothing to see and nothing to chew
Some think that nothing day is really nice
Not me! I d rather _____

Add and illustrate two additional verses.

January 17

Birthday of Benjamin Franklin 1706-1790

Besides being one of the important figures in Revolutionary times, Franklin was responsible for many firsts: the first wood heating stove, the first eyeglasses, the first street lights, the first public library and the first fire department are but a few. As an inventor he combined things he had available in new ways to meet a specific need.

Suppose you needed an **invention** to water house plants while the family is on vacation. Combine at least four of these things to create an automatic house plant waterer. Write a **description** of how the invention works.

20 pound weight	an empty bottle	a length of hose	a tire
a candle	a springboard	a rope	a match
rubber bands	paper cups	faucet	a pitcher

January 18

Birthday of Peter Mark Roget 1779-1869

The thesaurus developed by this man is every writer's companion. It gives multiple words with similar meanings to stretch vocabulary and enhance description.

Choose a favorite TV, movie or book character._____

Write one word that best describes this character. _____

Use the thesaurus to find other words with similar meanings. Write a **paragraph describing** the character. Use as many words from the thesaurus as you can.

January 19

Birthday of Edgar Allan Poe 1809-1849

Edgar Allan Poe was a writer of mystery and horror tales. Many of his stories have been made into films.

The Mystery Writers of America is an organization that presents an award to the author of the best mystery written each year. It is called the Edgar Allan Poe Award.

Of all the mystery books you have read, to which would you give the Edgar Allan Poe Award?

List the title and author of the book and write a short **paragraph explaining** why it should receive the award.

January 20

The Disappearing Town

You and your family earn your living by traveling around the Old West in a covered wagon putting on magic shows. You are headed for Cactus City where you have sent handbills telling about the show. There are no road signs showing the way, but you spot a church steeple from the trail. When you arrive you find a neat, freshly painted town, but no people. The only living creature is a very thirsty dog that does tricks.

Where is everyone? What happened to them? Put your imagination to work and continue the **story**. Tell what your theatrical troop will do now and how you can find out what happened to the townsfolk. Share your story with your class.

After writing your version you may want to read *Mr. Mysterious and Company* by Sid Fleischman.

January 21

Animal Detectives

Imagine you are trying to **solve a mystery**. You will be assisted by an animal.

A) What animal would you choose? _____

B) What detective traits does this animal have? _____

_____

C) What could this animal do that you could not? _____

_____

D) How could this animal get information that would not be available to you?

_____

_____

Read any or all of the *Sebastian, Super Sleuth* mysteries by Mary Blount Christian.

JANUARY 22

TAKE A LETTER DAY

GOOD GUYS	BAD GUYS
1.	
2.	
3.	
4.	
5.	

1. Write the names of five admirable characters from literature in the left hand column of the T.
2. Write the names of five unlikable characters in the right hand column of the T.
3. Choose a character from each column.
4. Write a **letter** of advice from one character you chose to the other. The advice should be needed and the letter should reveal something about each character.

January 23

Birthday of Humphrey Bogart 1899-1957

Humphrey Bogart was a leading film actor whose films are considered classics and often shown today. Use an almanac to **answer these questions**.

A. The title of one of his most famous films is a city in Africa.
   Name the film._____

B. Bogart won the Academy Award for Best Actor in 1951.
   What was the film?_____

C. Bogart's leading lady in his Academy Award film did not win the award that year.
   Who was she and what other years did she win the award?

   _____

D. **Write** one page nominating your favorite actor or actress for the Academy Award.
   Mention his/her films and give specific reasons why he or she deserves the award.

January 24

Gold Discovered in California 1848

The following headlines might have appeared in Western newspapers in the 1800s. Choose one topic to read about. **Write a news story** to accompany the headline. Be sure to tell what happened, when and where it happened and who was involved.

1. Gold Discovered at Sutter's Fort
2. Comstock Lode Richest Ever!
3. Railroad Crosses Entire United States
4. Wells Fargo Starts New Service
5. Pony Express Begins
6. Homestead Act Passed

January 25

Birthday of James Flora 1914

One of James Flora's tall tales is about a hen that will hatch anything put in her nest. Flour in the nest hatches into a loaf of bread. A door knob becomes a new front door.

Suppose you were left in charge of the farm for a week. What would you give Little Hatchy Hen to hatch?

Write a tall tale about what you would give her, what hatched and what happened as a result.

January 26

Tap Dancing Record Broken

On this date in 1998 Michael Flatley, dancing star of Riverdance, broke the world's record for achieving the fastest rate in tap dancing. This happened in the Wembley Arena in London, England.

Here are the names of five other famous dancers. Research and **write three or four sentences** about each telling why they achieved greatness.

1. Maria Tallchief
2. Isadora Duncan
3. Katherine Dunham
4. Fred Astaire
5. Arthur Murray

January 27

Birthday of Lewis Carroll 1832-1898

In *Alice In Wonderland* this author created many strange characters and situations. At one point Alice shrinks, becoming very tiny. In this state she feels quite helpless. Tiny things, however, can do amazing things.

A grasshopper can jump twenty times its body length. If you had this ability how far could you jump?

An ant can lift fifty times its weight. If you had this ability, how many pounds could you lift?

Create a **short fantasy story** where you can jump twenty times your height and lift fifty times your weight. What would you be able to do? What would others think or say about your unusual abilities? In what ways could you use these abilities to help others?

January 28

Birthday of Vera B. Williams 1927

One of Ms. Williams' most popular books is the picture book *A Chair for My Mother*. In this story a girl named Rosa helps save money to buy a big comfortable chair for her hard-working mother.

Write a story about something you would like to have but do not have enough money to buy. How would you earn the money? Think of some unusual ways. Let your reader share your feelings when you are finally able to purchase the item.

January 29

First Football Hall of Fame Members Selected

In 1963 the first members of the Football Hall of Fame were chosen, You can visit the Hall of Fame in Canton, Ohio, and learn more about these football heroes. **Nominate** three current players for the Hall of Fame. **Give your reasons** for each nomination. Who would you choose from these positions and why?

Center	Quarterback	Left Halfback
Left Guard	Right Guard	Right Halfback
Left Tackle	Right Tackle	Fullback
Left End	Right End	

January 30

A Fateful Day

January 30th was a fateful day in the lives of three world leaders. The day was significant to each for very different reasons.

Investigate and prepare a **short report** telling why January 30th was so important to:

A) Franklin D. Roosevelt   President of the United States

B) Adolf Hitler   German leader: World War II

C) Mohandas Gandhi   Religious leader: India

January 31

Birthday of Gerald McDermott 1941

As an animated film maker Gerald McDermott was puzzled as to how to bring a story to life in a book where there was no movement, music or sound effects. In his award winning *Arrow To the Sun* he met these challenges by using rich colors to fill large areas and a rainbow trail motif to move the reader's eye across the page. Find and read *Arrow to the Sun*. Create an **acrostic book report**. Retell the story using the letters in the title to begin the first word of each line.

A_____
R_____
R_____
O_____
W_____

T_____
O_____

T_____
H_____
E_____

S_____
U_____
N_____

February 1

Black History Month

This entire month is devoted to the study of black history in many schools in the United States. **Discover** the achievement of each of these famous black Americans.

Crispus Attucks
Elijah McCoy
Jackie Robinson
Thurgood Marshall

Harriet Tubman
Martin Luther King, Jr.
Marian Anderson
Maya Angelou

Frederick Douglass
Langston Hughes
Matthew Henson
Jesse Owens

February 2

Groundhog Day

Legend says that the groundhog awakens every February 2nd from hibernation. If the sun is shining he goes back to sleep causing six more weeks of winter. **Answer these questions**.

1. This legend was brought to America from what two countries?
_____   _____
2. Another name for groundhog is _____
3. Check the weather today. Will there, according to legend, be six more weeks of winter?
_____. Why?_____
_____

February 3

First Cotton Mill Opens 1789

Cotton has long been an important U.S. Crop. Use an almanac to find the five leading cotton producing states. **List** them from the largest to the smallest producer.

1._____

2._____

3._____

4._____

5._____

February 4

Navy Distinguished Service Medal Authorized 1919

This medal is awarded by the Navy to one who gives exceptional service in a duty of great responsibility. What great United States Naval heroes or heroines who lived before 1919 would deserve this medal? Tell why.

_____ should receive the Navy Distinguished Service Medal because _____

_____

February 5

First Performance of the Opera *Boris Godunov* 1874

This popular Mussorgsky opera was first performed in St. Petersburg, Russia. The story is based on the famous historic attempt by a young monk to impersonate the murdered Prince Dimitre and lead a revolution against Czar Boris Godunov, the prince's murderer.

Listen to music from this opera or from other works by Mussorgsky. How would you **describe** his music? **Choose a poem** that has the same mood as the music. Read the poem aloud to your class while playing the music.

February 6

Animal Collectives

Learn new words today. Check an encyclopedia or dictionary to **match** the animals that belong in each group.

1. a cete of	A) cattle
2. a drove of	B) bees
3. a gam of	C) badgers
4. a grist of	D) kangaroos
5. a knot of	E) toads
6. a mob of	F) whales

Create a **poster** to show what you have learned.

February 7

Birthday of Laura Ingalls Wilder 1867-1957

Laura Ingalls Wilder described pioneer life vividly in her "Little House" books. Read *Little House on the Prairie* or *Little House in the Big Woods*. Use information from the book to write a **Recipe for A Pioneer**. Share your recipe with your class.

Ingredients

_____
_____
_____
_____

Directions

_____
_____
_____
_____

February 8

Boy Scouts of America Founded 1910

A Boy Scout Quiz

1. At what age can one become a Boy Scout?_____

2. What are the three levels of the program? _____
_____

3. Who fostered the organization in the United States? _____
_____

4. Who was the first United States Scout Commissioner? _____
_____

5. What are the major aims of the Boy Scouts?

_____

_____

_____

_____

February 9

Gasparilllillo Pirate Invasion (Tampa, Florida)

(movable date)

This festival celebrates the exploits of the Spanish Pirate José Gaspar. There have been many famous pirates throughout history, some real and others fictional.

Underline the names of those pirates who really lived.

A) Barbarossa	C) Captain Hook	E) Ali Pichinin	G) Captain Kidd
B) Bluebeard	D) Khairr-ed-Di	F) Jean Lafittee	H) Blackbeard

February 10

Birthday of E. L. Konigsberg 1930

E. L. Konigsberg won the Newbery Medal for her book *From the Mixed Up Files of Mrs. Basil E. Frankweiler*. In the book we learn about the famous artist and sculptor, Michelangelo.
Answer the questions below to fill in the blanks and get a portrait of this great Renaissance artist.

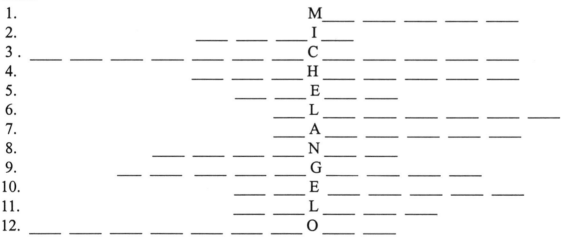

1. What Italian family helped Michelangelo?
2. Which work was carved from flawed marble in 1504?
3. Where did he paint "The Creation" and "The Last Judgment?"
4. Besides being a painter and sculptor, what other type of artist was he?
5. Which sculpture did he do several of, the most famous of which is in Rome?
6. In what Italian city other than Rome did he work and study?
7. In what Italian town was he born?
8. Michelangelo knew the artist who painted the "Mona Lisa." Who was he?
9. Who broke Michelangelo's nose?
10. What are paintings done on wet plaster called?
11. Which Pope commissioned Michelangelo to paint "The Creation" and "The Last Judgment?"
12. What was Michelangelo's surname?

February 11

Birthday of Thomas Edison 1847-1931

This prolific inventor showed little promise in his early life. He had great difficulty in school and was finally taken out of school and taught at home by his mother.

Read about the childhood of Thomas Edison. Write a **letter** from his third grade teacher explaining to his parents why he needed to repeat the third grade.

List five inventions by Thomas Edison that are used today. **Rank order** your list from the one you think is most important to the least important. **Give reasons** for your first choice.

February 12

Birthday of Abraham Lincoln 1809-1864

Read *Abraham Lincoln* by Ingri and Edgar d' Aulaire. **Complete** the missing information below.
1. Abe's mother made this as a special treat._____
2. Abe split rails with this. _____
3. Abe carried papers in this._____
4. Abe was born in this kind of house._____
5. Abe's school had no chairs or desks, just_____
6. Abe's school book looked like a _____.

February 13

First American Magazine Published 1741

This first magazine for adults was called *The American Magazine*. It expressed political views and lasted three months. Today magazines are available for every age and about nearly every topic of interest. Look at the periodical section of your library.

Which magazine is the most unusual?_____

Take a **poll** of your classmates. List the favorite magazine of each.

Which magazine did boys mention most? _____

Which magazine did girls mention most? _____

Which magazine was mentioned more than any other by all students?_____

February 14

Birthday of George Shannon 1952

George Shannon, a children's librarian and professional storyteller, strongly believes in the continuation of the oral storytelling tradition. Since Valentine's Day is George Shannon's birthday, celebrate by **telling a cumulative tale**. Begin the tale with a toad with a tiny red heart on his belly who jumps into George's left shirt pocket. Each person, in turn, will tell how George tried to get rid of the toad but how the toad with a heart always finds its way back. The last person in the group must present a unique solution for George and his pocket pal. Groups of five or six make the story just long enough.

February 15

Susan B. Anthony Day

Why is this day set aside to remember this great woman? _____
_____

Here are other famous women. In which field did each achieve fame?

1. Phyllis Wheatley_____
2. Elizabeth Stanton_____
3. Harriet Tubman _____
4. Theresa Cori _____
5. Geraldine Ferraro_____

February 16

PTA Organized 1897

Find out about your school's parent-teacher organization.

1. Who is the president? _____

2. When does it meet? _____

3. What is the major purpose of the organization? _____

4. What special plans does the organization have for the rest of this school year?
_____
_____
_____
_____

February 17

Nylon Patented 1937

Investigate where these materials come from.

1. Nylon _____

2. Wool _____

3. Cotton _____

4. Linen _____

5. Name one very important use of nylon in World War II.

_____

February 18

Jefferson Davis Inaugurated 1861

Jefferson Davis served as President of the Confederate States of America during the Civil War.

Below are important events in Davis's life. Place the number of each in its correct place on the **time line**.

1. Graduated United States Military Academy

2. Won the Battle of Buena Vista

3. Secretary of War

4. President of the Confederacy

5. Married the daughter of Zachary Taylor

6. Elected United States Representative

7. Elected to the United States Senate

_____
1828   1835   1845   1846   1853   1862

February 19

Tintype Camera Patented 1856

Compile a **photo essay**. It is said that one picture equals a thousand words. Follow a current news event for one week or longer. Collect newspaper photographs of the event. Caption the photographs and display them in chronological order. How well do they tell the story?

Explain the event to your class using the photographs. Be prepared to answer questions about the event.

February 20

John Glenn Orbits the Earth 1962

John H. Glenn, Jr. was the first American to orbit the Earth. His spacecraft made three complete revolutions around the Earth. On the flight Glenn saw strange sights which he described in an almost poetic manner.

Brainstorm all the space words you can. Use them in a **poem**. Follow the diamente pattern below.

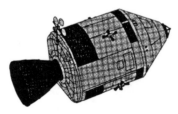

Alien
Strange, frightening
UFO, Spaceship, Starward
Eerie, Distant, Traveler, Searcher
Omniscient, Contact, Encounter
Hope, Direction
Alien

February 21

Washington Monument Dedicated 1885

Complete the missing words in this paragraph.
This monument has the shape of the A)_____ of ancient Egypt.
It is B)_____high. The walls are covered with white C)_____
from D)_____.
Visitors must take an E)_____ to the top of the monument where
they see an impressive view of F)_____
The monument is maintained by G)_____.

February 22

Birthday of George Washington 1732-1799

Write a **cinquain** to honor George Washington on his birthday.

Line One (one word)   Leader

Line Two (two adjectives)   _____ _____

Line Three (three verbs) _____ _____ _____

Line Four (four words) _____ _____ _____ _____

Line Five (Synonym)   _____

February 23

Rotary Club Founded 1905

Every community has one or more organizations whose purpose is to make the community a better place to live. **Survey** your community. **List** and give the purpose of three organizations.

1. _____ Purpose_____

2. _____ Purpose_____

3. _____ Purpose_____

Select an organization and **interview** a member. What project does the organization sponsor for community betterment?

_____

February 24

Birthday of Chester Nimitz 1885-1966

Admiral Nimitz served as commander-in-chief of the U.S. Pacific fleet in World War II. **Answer these questions.**

1. In the early months of the War he made Congressmen angry because_____

2. He developed the strategy of _____
   seizing only key islands from which to launch attacks.

3. Nimitz _____ for the United States at the Japanese surrender ceremonies in Tokyo Bay.

February 25

Colt Pistol Patented 1836

Samuel Colt developed the first successful repeating pistol which later became known as the six shooter. These men became infamous as a result of their use of Colt's weapon. Many movies have been made about them. Can you **name** them?

1. J ___ ___ ___ ___   J ___ ___ ___ ___

2. D ___ ___   H ___ ___ ___ ___ ___ ___ ___

3. B ___ ___ ___ ___ the K ___ ___

Define infamous. _____

_____

February 26

Birthday of William F. Cody 1846-1917

Identify the occupations Cody had during his life.

A) Livestock handler	G) railroad worker
B) Team driver	H) Buffalo hunter
C) Pony Express rider	I) Guide
D) Scout	J) Indian fighter
E) Hotel operator	K) Showman
F) Freight handler	L) Rancher

February 27

Birthday of Henry W. Longfellow 1807-1882

Many of Longfellow's poems are read and enjoyed today. Find and read one of these poems to your class. Consider **recording** your reading with appropriate background music.
Among Longfellow's most famous poems are:

"The Village Blacksmith"
"Paul Revere's Ride"
"The Wreck of the Hesperus"

February 28

First Killer Whale Born In Captivity 1977

This whale was born in Marineland in Los Angeles and created considerable excitement. Whales have always been of interest to humans. One classic tale, *Moby Dick*, by Herman Melville tells of the pursuit of a great white whale by a mad ship's captain.

Some species of whales are endangered today. One of these is the blue whale which is the largest animal in the world.

List eight products that come from whales.

1. _____   5. _____
2. _____   6. _____
3. _____   7. _____
4. _____   8. _____

February 29

Leap Year

Since you have an extra day this year, what better way to spend it than curled up with a good book. Try one of these.

Gregory, Kristiana. ***Orphan Runaways.*** Scholastic, 1998. Gr 4-6
In 1878 Danny and Judd run away from a miserable orphanage in San Francisco, and thus begins an exciting adventure set in a gold rush boom town.
Activity Find out what the following would cost in San Francisco at the beginning of the gold rush (1849): 1 dozen eggs, 1 loaf of bread, 1 pound of butter, needle and thread, a shovel. (A good source of information is Rhonda Blumberg's *Great American Gold Rush.*)

Hill, Donna. ***Shipwreck Season.*** Clarion, 1998. Gr 5-8
Young Daniel spends eight months among rough seamen at a lifesaver's station but gains respect for those who risk their lives to save others in this 1880s story.
Activity Research and write ten clues about someone connected with the sea. One clue must be a give-away clue. Ask classmates to give you a number between one and ten. Read the clue. The student can guess or pass. The game continues until the person is guessed or all clues are read.

Lasky, Kathryn. ***Alice Rose & Sam.*** Hyperion, 1998. Gr 4-7
A gritty silver mining town, a young girl, crooked judges, and a murder all make for an exciting tale of the days of the Comstock Lode when Alice Rose and Samuel Clemens team up to foil the plans of the mysterious Society of Seven.
Activity Summarize the story using the title as the first letters of each line.

March 1

Major Railroad Disaster, Wellington, WA 1910

With ninety-six deaths this was one of the major railroad accidents in United States history. Throughout World War II passenger trains were a major means of transportation throughout the country. Airlines have since taken first place in mass long distance travel.

Research these events in the history of the railroad.

1. Circle the key word in each statement. Use the resources of the library or the Internet to identify these famous railroad men.

   A) The man who built the first locomotive, the *Tom Thumb*, which lost its first race with a stagecoach

   _____

   B) The first crude steam engine was built in England in 1705 by

   _____

   C) The father of the modern locomotive is

   _____

   D) The first U.S. President to ride on a train was

   _____

2. Check the encyclopedia or a book about trains to **match** each term with its meaning.

   _____ 1. car knocker   A. pick up speed
   _____ 2. crummy   B. clear signal
   _____ 3. drag   C. car inspector
   _____ 4. green eye   D. caboose
   _____ 5. highball   E. temporary track
   _____ 6. redball   F. refrigerator car
   _____ 7. reefer   G. slow freight car
   _____ 8. shoofly   H. fast freight train

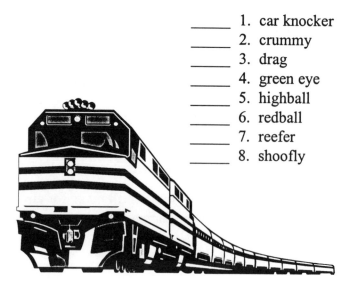

March 2

Texas Independence Day

On March 2, 1836, Texas declared its independence from Mexico. Nine years later in 1845 Texas was annexed by the United States and later that year became a state. **Identify** what part each of these men played in these events.

1) Stephen Austin _____
2) Antonio Lopez de Santa Anna _____
3) Sam Houston _____
4) John Tyler _____

March 3

Alexander Graham Bell Day 1847-1922

While Alexander Graham Bell is best known for the invention of the telephone, he has a variety of other inventions to his credit as well. **Circle** below those inventions that can be credited to Bell. **List** at least two present day uses for the inventions you circle.

photophone	tetrahedral kite
phonograph	aileron
audiometer	hydrofoil speedboat

March 4

U. S. Government Printing Office Opens 1861

The United States Government is the largest publisher in the nation, printing millions of books and pamphlets on a wide variety of subjects.

Major publishers have LOGOS to easily identify their books. Look for publishers' logos on books in the library.

Design a logo for the United States Government Printing Office.

March 5

Boston Massacre 1768

Complete this news account.

On March 5, 1768, _____ of the king's soldiers were pelted with _____ by a group of angry citizens. The soldiers opened fire resulting in the deaths of Boston patriots. The first to be killed was _____ _____, a former slave. This outrage was denounced in a mass meeting which demanded the removal of _____ troops from

_____.

March 6

# Alamo Day (Fall of the Alamo 1836)

Read about the fall of the Alamo. **Complete** this narrative poem by filling in the blank lines.

In eighteen hundred thirty six
Some Texans took a stand.
They gathered in the Alamo
To defend _____

Their leaders who would show no fear

_____

They fought for rights that they held dear

_____

March 7

Peter Pan Telecast 1955

This was a much-watched television special with the original Broadway cast of the classic story of the boy who did not want to grow up.

Imagine that you could choose one age and remain at that age for all of your life. **List** the advantages and disadvantages of being one age year after year. Age _____

Advantages	Disadvantages
_____	_____
_____	_____
_____	_____
_____	_____
_____	_____

March 8

Fishing Rod Patented 1887

Match these top fishing lakes with the state in which each is located.

1) Lake of the Ozarks _____
2) Toledo Bend _____
3) Greer's Ferry _____
4) Thousand Islands _____
5) Lake Mead _____

A) Arkansas
B) New York
C) Missouri
D) Nevada
E) Texas

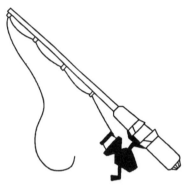

March 9

Birthday of Edwin Forrest 1806-1872

Edwin Forrest was the first American actor to be recognized internationally. He played in both the United States and London and was popular for almost fifty years. Unfortunately the Tony Awards given for the best plays and actors were not established in Forrest's day.

Use an almanac to see who won the Tony Award as the best dramatic actor in the year you were born.

Year _____   Actor _____

Name two plays or motion pictures in which this actor appeared.

_____   _____

March 10

First Dental School Established 1869

Professors at this first dental school would be astounded at the amazing things dentists can do today. **Read** about modern dentistry. **List** as many procedures as you can that dentists can perform today that they could not perform in 1869.

_____

_____

Create a **poster** showing how to keep teeth and gums healthy.

March 11

Blizzard of the Year 1888

This famous blizzard isolated New York City from the nation and still serves as the basis for many tall tales.

Example: It was so cold that words froze in the air, and no one knew what anybody said until the spring thaw.

Write and **illustrate** several tall tale weather statements of your own:

1. It was so cold that ...   4. It was so _____
2. It rained so hard that...   5. It was so _____
3. It was so hot that ...   6. It was so _____

March 12

Girl Scouts Founded 1912

Founded by Juliette Low, the Girl Scouts have as their purposes to develop citizenship, service, health and character. Suppose the Girl Scouts gave awards to literary characters for demonstrating each of these qualities. What character would you **nominate** for each award? Give a **reason** for each nomination.

	Character	Reason
1. Citizenship		
2. Service		
3. Health		
4. Character		

March 13

Death of Clarence Darrow 1857-1938

Read about the life of this famous lawyer. Use the formula below to **explain** why he was so opposed to prejudice and bigotry.

Motivating Forces + Resources

+ Immediate Physical Setting

= Behavior

1. What motivated Darrow to oppose bigotry?

2. What resources did he have to use in the fight against prejudice?

3. What was the time in which he lived?

4. What did he do?

March 14

Birthday of Albert Einstein 1879-1955

Einstein was considered to be one of the most intellectually gifted persons who ever lived.

Below are some statements often heard about gifted persons. Read about Einstein's life and give a **reason** why each statement is true or not true as it applies to Einstein.

1. Gifted people show their unusual gifts early in life.

2. Early giftedness burns out later in life.

3. Gifted people do not do well in school.

4. Gifted people are physically weak and often sickly.

5. Gifted people do not communicate well with other people.

Name three gifted people that you feel do **not** represent the statements above.

_____   _____   _____

March15

First Practical Use of Rockets 1926

Robert Goddard's first rocket traveled 184 feet in two and one half seconds. Since this first rocket demonstration, many uses have been found for rockets. Below are several important events based on rocketry. **Match** the spacecraft with the event. Use an almanac for help.

1) _____ Sputnik   A) First American in space

2) _____ Mercury-Redstone III   B) First walk in space

3) _____ Mercury-Atlas VI   C) Man walks on the moon

4) _____ Gemini-Titan IV   D) First American in orbit

5) _____ Apollo-Saturn X   E) First man in space

March 16

Birthday of Sid Fleischman 1920

Sid Fleishman is best known as a teller of tall tales. Among his books are *By the Great Horn Spoon, Ghost in the Noonday Sun, Humbug Mountain, The Whipping Boy* and the *McBroom* series.

In tall tales the idea of bigness is important. In the sentences that follow are some unusual ways of relating to the concept of *big*. Look at the underlined words. Do you know these words? Look them up in an unabridged dictionary to **define** their exact meaning and their derivation (where the word comes from).

1. Pecos Bill is a hero of <u>Gargantuan</u> proportions.

_____

_____

2. Stormalong is America s <u>Cyclopean</u> hero.

_____

_____

3. John Henry's steel-driving power was <u>Titanic</u>.

_____

_____

4. Everything about Paul Bunyan tales is <u>Brobdingnagian</u>.

_____

_____

5. Joe Magarac was a man of <u>Herculean</u> size.

_____

_____

March 17

St. Patrick's Day

Legend says that St. Patrick drove all the snakes from Ireland. Read about his life.
Complete the missing information in items one through four. Do you think the legend is true? Why or why not?

1. Patrick was born in _____
2. He was captured and sold as a _____
3. He became Patron Saint of _____
4. A well-known sign of St. Patrick's Day is _____

March 18

Major Tornados Hit Missouri, Illinois and Indiana 1925

Answer these questions about tornadoes.

A. An average tornado is about _____ feet across.
B. An average strong tornado's winds blow about _____ to _____ miles per hour.
C. The average tornado sweeps a path at a speed of _____ to _____ miles per hour.

Create a **poster** telling what action people should take when tornado warnings are issued.

March 19

Tall Tale Messages

One of the following tall tale heroes has called and left a message. **Compose a message** that would be helpful to the person receiving it in solving his or her basic problem. Tell who is sending and who is receiving the message.

Message Senders	Message Receivers
Paul Bunyan	Robinson Crusoe
Davy Crockett	Ebenezer Scrooge
Mike Fink	Rapunzel
Johnny Appleseed	Snow White
Pecos Bill	Gulliver
John Henry	Captain Hook

March 20

Birthday of Mitsumasa Anno 1926

This Japanese artist is known world-wide for his creative and beautiful books. One which is a feast for the eyes is *Anno's Flea Market*. In this wordless picture book the imagination is set free as one wanders through a great town square on a Saturday viewing stalls overflowing with things old and new, treasures and trash. After an optical feast, select three items that you would find worthless. On separate slips of paper write the name of each item. Put the slips in a jar and ask a classmate to draw out a slip and **tell** how the item on that slip could be a treasure. What uses could the item serve?

March 21

Philatelic Society Established 1867

Stamp collecting can be a fascinating hobby. Collectors enjoy getting together to trade and admire stamps. Recently the Postal Service has begun issuing stamps honoring well-known twentieth century Americans.

Take a class **poll**. Make a list of five outstanding twentieth century Americans you believe should be honored by having their images on postage stamps. Total the scores.

The winner is _____

Write a letter to the U.S. Postal Service nominating the winner for a stamp. Give reasons why you and your classmates feel this person should be honored.

March 22

First Indian Treaty 1621

This first treaty was signed in 1621 by Governor John Carver of Plymouth Colony and Massasoit. In 1683, William Penn met with Tamanend, Chief of the Delaware Indians, to sign a treaty known as the Great Treaty. Unfortunately, these and many other treaties made with Native Americans were not honored.

Compile a **scrapbook** of famous Eastern Indian leaders. Find information from the encyclopedia, books and the Internet. Leaders to consider for inclusion are:

Massasoit	Tamanend	Hiawatha
Sequoyah	Techumseh	

March 23

Patrick Henry's Speech for Liberty 1775

Patrick Henry was a very dramatic speaker. At a provincial convention in Virginia, Henry introduced a resolution calling for a militia. He grabbed a knife-shaped letter opener and pretending to plunge it into his heart shouted, *"As for me, give me liberty or give me death."*

To learn more about Patrick Henry and other famous men of his time, read one or more of these books by Jean Fritz. Create a **poster** to interest classmates in reading the book.

Where Was Patrick Henry On the 29th of May?

Why Don't You Get A Horse, John Adams?

And Then What Happened, Paul Revere?

What's The Big Idea, Ben Franklin?

Will You Sign Here, John Hancock?

March 24

Twisted Nursery Rhymes

This form of **poetry** is not new to you, but it is different. Take the first line of a favorite nursery rhyme, add imagination and create three new facts about the character(s). Line one rhymes with line two and line three rhymes with line four.

Here is an example to help you get started.

Jack be nimble, Jack be quick   _____

Do you know why he did that trick?   _____

He did not jump. He was not tripped.   _____

Was on a banana peel he slipped.   _____

March 25

Birthday of Gloria Steinem 1934

For what is Gloria Steinem best known?

_____

What is the claim to fame of each of these women?

1. Molly Pitcher _____
2. Elizabeth Blackwell _____
3. Margaret Chase Smith _____
4. Sally Ride _____

March 26

Birthday of Sandra Day O'Connor 1930

Sandra Day O'Connor is the first woman to serve as a Supreme Court Justice.

Find out how each of these women were FIRST.

1. Susan B. Anthony_____
2. Wilma Rudolph _____
3. Maria Mitchell _____
4. Pearl S. Buck _____
5. Jeannette Rankin _____

March 27

Alaska Earthquake 1964

This great earthquake measured 8.4 on the Richter Scale and destroyed most of downtown Anchorage. Since then the town has been rebuilt in the same place despite the danger of future quakes.

Find out about the major earthquake zones in the United States. Mark these zones on a **map**. More earthquakes occur in California than any other state. Find and **list reasons** why this is true.

1. Is it possible another Alaskan earthquake could occur?_____
2. How are earthquakes measured? _____
3. What causes earthquakes? _____

March 28

Major Nuclear Accident
Three Mile Island, Pennsylvania 1979

On this day the news announcers in the area surrounding Three Mile Island tried to maintain a manner of calm assurance even though the danger of the nuclear accident was not fully known. If there was a meltdown (which fortunately, there was not), the entire area would be flooded with radiation. Highways would be jammed with people trying to escape. Panic could well lead to violence.

Environmental hazards are of two types: (1) Those which are immediate and short range in effect. (2) Those more distant, more devastating, a threat to life itself.

The seriousness of an environmental disaster is determined by those it affects. The ranking is as follows (1) person (2) family (3) community (4) region or nation (5) several regions or nations (6) civilization (7) human species (8) Earth (9) solar system (10) Universe

Rank these environmental disasters as to type one or type two and for the degree of seriousness 1-10.

Disaster	Type	Degree of Seriousness
Sinking of the Titanic	_____	_____
Tornadoes in Iowa	_____	_____
London Plague	_____	_____
Love Canal Contamination	_____	_____
Drought in Africa	_____	_____
Eruption of Mt. St. Helens	_____	_____
Three Mile Island accident	_____	_____
San Francisco earthquake	_____	_____
Hurricane Camille	_____	_____
Dioxin contamination, Times Beach, MO	_____	_____

March 29

Imagine An Author

Fill in the information about a favorite author as you think it might be.

Name_____ Age_____

Married?_____ Works at home?_____

Tall?_____ Short?_____

Number of Children_____

Favorite Hobby _____

Read about this author in *Something About the Author* (Gale Series) to support or deny your guesses.

March 30

Seward's Day (Alaska)

This day celebrates the purchase of Alaska from Russia in 1867 for seven million dollars.

1) Figuring a modest inflation rate of 5% per year, what would be the purchase price today? _____

2) Is this price still a bargain? Defend your answer.

_____

_____

_____

_____

March 31

Birthdays of Herb Alpert 1935
Richard Chamberlain 1935 Shirley Jones 1934

Check the *Reader's Guide* or the Internet for information about these three entertainers. Each share the same zodiac sign, Aries, which astrologers say give them similar personalities.

A) What major personality traits would an Aries person be expected to have?

_____

B) Do any of the above entertainers fit the Aries personality? Explain.

_____

_____

April 1

April Fools Day

What a great day to read a book about people who were fooled! Try one of these or find and review another tale for your classmates about someone who was fooled.

Wright, Betty Ren. *A Ghost in the Family.* Scholastic, 1998. Gr 4-6
Chad vacations in a boarding house full of odd characters...a mummy appears, a panther leaps out of his closet, a fortune-teller predicts trouble and a diamond bracelet is stolen.
Activity   Describe a strange character you might create if you were to write a boarding house story.

Yep, Laurence. *The Imp That Ate My Homework*. HarperCollins, 1998. Gr 4-7
Jim discovers that his Grandpop has the ability to turn himself into a supernatural warrior when a nasty green imp appears. Together they face the imp in a wild battle of magic and wits.
Activity   Write an excuse for not having your homework. Include at least three of these items in the excuse: a firecracker, a crazed deer, a strong wind, a jar of peanut butter, a one-eyed cat, a magnet, a table with one leg, a bucket of water, a cracked sidewalk, an alarm clock.

April 2

Birthday of Dr. Seuss

In this paragraph are titles of many books by this favorite author. **Underline** all those you can find.

One day the Lorax met Yertle the turtle on the way to McElligot s pool. *"Did I ever tell you how lucky you are?"* asked the Lorax. *"And to think I saw it on Mulberry Street! The sign was six feet high and said, 'Happy birthday to you.' Now everyone knows why you had scrambled eggs super for breakfast and then borrowed the king's stilts to take a walk. I know a cat in a hat who did not have as happy a birthday as you."*

April 3

First Pony Express Run 1860

The first cross country mail traveled by teams on horseback 1,980 miles between Sacramento, California, and St. Joseph, Missouri.

To accomplish this feat took much planning to be sure a fresh horse and rider was ready when the mail arrived at each station.

Here are some make believe rules which might have been posted at the stations.

1. Beds available on a first come, first served basis. No more than four gentlemen to a bed. Charge: 25 cents per night.

2. Spurs, boots and gun belts, including gun, must be removed before retiring.

3. Dogs may sleep in the room with their owners but not in the bed. Other riders may object to sleeping with dogs.

4. All beds must be empty by seven a.m. This is important as sheets are used as tablecloths.

5. Towels must not be removed from the room. One towel is provided for each four guests. Towels are changed once a month, if necessary.

6. No spitting on the walls or floor.

7. No complaining about the food. You must eat what is served or go hungry. Attacks on the cook are strictly forbidden.

8. If a guest finds his baggage thrown out on the street he can assume that the mail has arrived and he'd better get moving to the next station.

Be in charge! Research! What rules would you post if you were:

1. Captain of a pirate ship in the Caribbean in 1850
2. Leader of a wagon train on the Oregon Trail in 1860
3. Commander of a space flight
4. Teacher in a one room school in 1900
5. Leader of the Beatles rock group on tour in the United States in 1965

April 4

Flag Act of 1818

The United States Flag has seen many changes since the original thirteen stars and stripes. Do you know the meaning of the stars? The stripes? The colors?

Design a flag that represents one special group in our country. This might be for the handicapped, the elderly, children or any group you choose.

Explain the symbols and colors used in your flag.

April 5

A Spring Ghost Story

You are a young child growing up near St. Louis one hundred years ago. Your mother disapproves of your friendship with Blossom Culp, the daughter of the local fortune teller. You discover (1) that a ghost lives in your barn (2) that the ghost cannot rest until taken to its final resting place in New Orleans (3) the only adult who believes you is your uncle and your mother disapproves of him as well. What will your course of action be to rid your barn of the ghost?

Read *The Ghost Belonged to Me* by Richard Peck and its sequel *Ghosts I Have Been* to learn more about this boy and his problems.

April 6

North Pole Reached 1909

After twenty-five years of effort, the North Pole was reached by a team of men from three races. **Answer these questions**.

Who were they? What race did each represent?

1. _____

2. _____

3. _____

April 7

The Good Old Days

Compare your life to that of a child living in rural America in the 1930s.

	THEN	NOW
1. Chores	_____	_____
2. School	_____	_____
3. Entertainment	_____	_____
4. Ambitions	_____	_____

April 8

Juan Ponce deLeon Claims Florida for Spain 1513

Suppose Florida belonged to Spain today. **List** as many **differences** as you can between a Spanish-owned Florida and your state.

FLORIDA	MY STATE
_____	_____
_____	_____
_____	_____
_____	_____
_____	_____
_____	_____
_____	_____

April 9

Where Did They Originate?

Many things we use everyday actually originated in other parts of the world. **Identify** the origin of the following by using **A** for America, **E** for England, **C** for China and **G** for Greece.

1. clock	_____	5. elevator	_____
2. soccer	_____	6. train	_____
3. safety pin	_____	7. paper	_____
4. Olympic Games	_____	8. zipper	_____

April 10

Salvation Army Founders Day

Research the work of the Salvation Army. Finish this **alliterative paragraph** with facts you discover. As many words as possible in your paragraph should begin with the letter **S**.

The Salvation Army saves many souls by serving sandwiches. _____

_____

_____

_____

_____

April 11

Jackie Robinson Joins the Brooklyn Dodgers 1947

Jackie Robinson was the first African-American to play with a major team. An acronym for him might be FIB (First In Brooklyn). Acronyms spell words and are usually the names of organizations. Research the accomplishments of these players. What might the **acronym** mean?

1. Lou Brock belongs to R.U.N.

_____

2. Reggie Jackson is a member of H.I.T.

_____

3. Catfish Hunter is eligible for F.O.U.L.

_____

4. Mark McGwire belongs to H.O.M.E.

_____

April 12

Birthday of Hardie Gramatky 1907

Hardie Gramatky is the author of *Little Toot*. This book was so popular that other Little Toot books followed placing Little Toot in various parts of the world. Read these clues.

Name the river that Little Toot is navigating.

1. This river is 3900 hundred miles long, the world's largest.
_____

2. This river is 4132 miles long, the world's longest.
_____

3. This river runs from Minnesota to the Gulf of Mexico.
_____

April 13

Sidney Poitier Wins Oscar 1963

Sidney Poitier was the first African-American actor to win the coveted award for best actor. **Find this information** in an almanac.

1. For what picture was he given the award?
_____

2. Did this film also win the Best Picture award that year?_____
3. Did Poitier win another Academy Award after 1963?_____
4. Who would you nominate for this year's Best Actor award?
_____

April 14

Sinking of the *Titanic* 1912

In his book *Great Mistakes* Lawrence Pringle says that mistakes are made due to
A) A lack of knowledge
B) Ignoring the facts
C) Taking a chance
D) Lack of planning

Read about the sinking of the *Titanic*. Which reason or reasons given above are responsible for the mistakes that were made? Support your answer with **evidence**.

April 15

Death of Abraham Lincoln 1864

Abraham Lincoln was admired for these qualities:

compassionate   dedicated   determined
honest   tireless   astute
shrewd   farsighted
pragmatic   empathetic

Read about Lincoln's life. Write a **short paragraph** about him in which you use six or more of these words.

April 16

Signs of the Times

For one week make **a list** of signs found in your community that regulate the behavior of people.

1. How many signs did you find? _____

2. Group the signs (hospital, library, street etc.) _____

3. Which signs, if any, do you feel are not needed? _____

4. Suggest new signs you feel are needed. _____

April 17

First Newspaper Published 1704

Since the publication of this first newspaper in Boston nearly every large city and small town has its own newspaper.

Examine a newspaper. **List** the various parts of the paper.

Create a *Fairy Tale Times* **Newspaper** in which you include top breaking stories, local news, a weather report, a social column, an editorial, a letter to the editor, cartoons, an advice column, want ads and any other features you want to add. Share your paper with the class.

April 18

San Francisco Earthquake 1906

This deadly earthquake killed more than 500 people. The resulting fire leveled the city.

When heat from the Earth's interior causes layers of earth to be squeezed and stretched, an earthquake is the result. In recent years scientists have found ways to harness geothermal energy but cannot with accuracy predict exactly when an earthquake will happen.

Read about and **define** three types of earthquake waves:

Primary _____

Secondary _____

Surface _____

April 19

Retell A Fable

Fables are easy to read because they are short. They are pleasant to read because they invoke a picture in your mind's eye. Fables are often amusing. Choose a favorite fable and change it into a **limerick**. Here is an example.

The Grasshopper and the Ants

There once were some hard-working ants
While grasshopper did nothing but dance
Each winter they'd feast
While hopper cried "Beasts!
My body slides off of my pants!"

April 20

Hot Springs National Park Established 1921

Native Americans were the first to use these mineral waters found in Arkansas. Hernando DeSoto discovered the springs in 1541. They are considered to be beneficial for some health problems.

A geyser such as Old Faithful in Yellowstone Park throws hot mineral water into the air. Old Faithful erupts for four minutes every sixty-five minutes.

Read about hot springs and geysers. Why don't the springs in Hot Springs National Park erupt?

_____

_____

_____

_____

April 21

National Gripers Day

There are many characters in literature who grumble and complain. Today is your chance to present the National Griper's Award. What literary character would you choose?

The National Griper's Award for the year _____ is presented to _____

_____ because _____

_____

April 22

First Earth Day 1970

Earth Day was established to help people become aware of their responsibility for taking care of the Earth that we all share.

Compile an *ABC Book* of taking care of Planet Earth. Share the book with your class.

Sample entries might be:
A is for . . . Always put your trash where it belongs.
B is for . . . Bike instead of ride.

April 23

A Big Country

Use an almanac to find these "superlative" **answers**.

1. Largest state _____
2. Northernmost city_____
3 Easternmost city_____
4. Longest river_____
5. Highest mountain _____
6. Tallest building_____
7. Highest bridge_____

April 24

Book of the Month Club Started 1926

The Book of the Month Club promotes the newest adult books published by sending a new book each month to members.

Suppose you were to start your own Book of the Month Club. **List** 12 of the best books you have read, one for each month of the year. Ask a friend to compile a similar list. **Compare** your lists. Do some of the same titles appear on each list? **List** three things that you feel make a book a good book.

_____
_____
_____

April 25

First License Plates Issued 1901

Since the first license plates were issued, personalized plates have become popular. A plate must have a combination of six numbers and/or letters. What plates would be appropriate for these well known people?

Example: Sandra Day O'Connor, Supreme Court Justice **(IRULE)**

Elizabeth Taylor_____
Rosa Parks_____
Coretta Scott King_____
Julia Roberts_____

April 26

Let's Eat Out Day!

Many foods we think of as American actually originated in other places in the world.

Identify the origin of:

1) beans   _____   A) Asia
2) olives   _____   B) Central/South America
3) apples   _____   C) Europe
4) sausage   _____   D) Middle East
5) chocolate   _____   E) America

April 27

What Word? Day

The best friend of every writer is a dictionary. It keeps the writer from overusing words and helps him or her to find better words in creating a character, setting, plot or mood.

Below you will find a paragraph from Hans Christian Anderson's *The Little Mermaid*. Many of the words Andersen chose to describe the bottom of the sea have been left out. Think of the most descriptive words you can to use in the blank spaces to create a picture for the reader. Use the dictionary to help you. Your **description** may be more vivid than Andersen's.

Now you must not think that on the bed of the ocean there is only white sand.

No, the most fantastic _____

and _____

grow there, with _____

and _____

so supple they respond to the _____

movement of the water. All the _____

and _____

fish glide in and out among the _____.

In the very deepest part lies the palace of the sea king. Its walls are made of _____

_____

The windows are of _____.

The roof consists of _____.

In front of the door are beautiful shells and in the center of each is a _____

_____.

April 28

Yellow Fever Vaccine Announced 1932

Walter Reed was the first to identify the yellow fever germ and its carrier, the mosquito. This led to the development of a preventive vaccine by Max Theiler.

There have been many famous firsts in the field of medicine. For what accomplishments are these men noted?

1. Joseph Lister_____
2. Henry Morton_____
3. Jonas Salk_____
4. Alexander Fleming_____

April 29

Literature Trivia Day

How well do you know folktales? Try this **quiz**.

A) Who only wanted a gift of a rose?
B) How many princesses wore their slippers out dancing every night?
C) What color was Rapunzel's hair?
D) Who danced in red shoes until she died?
E) Where did the Little Mermaid get human form?
F) What put Sleeping Beauty to sleep?
G) Who were the best known collectors of German fairy tales?

April 30

Seeing Eye Incorporated 1932

The Seeing Eye Organization provides guide dogs for the blind, enabling the blind person to become self-sufficient.

Many blind persons have become world famous. For what are these blind persons known?

1. Helen Keller _____
2. Ray Charles_____
3. George Shearing _____
4. Stevie Wonder _____
5. Alec Templeton _____

May 1

The Gift of a Lovely Thought

"If instead of a jewel, or even a flower, we could cast the gift of a lovely thought into the heart of another, that would be giving as the angels must give." Anonymous

What characters from literature can you name that best fit the famous quote above? **Name** three characters and the persons who received joy because of them.

1. _____
2. _____
3. _____

May 2

Kentucky Derby (Movable date)

Research horses under Dewey Number 636.1. **Match** these breeds with their jobs.

1. Thoroughbred   _____A. Army horse
2. Quarter Horse   _____B. Hauling logs
3. Australian Waler   _____C. Racing
4. Akhal-Teke   _____D. Rodeo Star
5. Ardennes   _____E. Russian sorting horse

Name the first recorded Derby winner in 1910. _____

May 3

First Medical School Opens 1865

Since this first United States medical school opened in Philadelphia there have been many significant medical discoveries. **Identify** the person given credit for each of these discoveries.

1. Understanding the process of digestion _____
2. Antiseptic surgery _____
3. Conquest of yellow fever _____
4. First U.S. heart transplant _____

May 4

Balloon Record Set 1961

Captain Malcolm Ross soared 113,739 feet to set a hot air balloon record for altitude. Ballooning has since become a major sport in the United States.

Find out if there are local balloonists in or near your community. **Interview** a balloonist. How is this sport different from other sports?

A good book about a balloonist is *Twenty-One Balloons* by William Pené Dubois. At one point in the story the balloonist has to make a fast escape because of an erupting volcano. How fast can a typical balloon rise?

May 5

Shepard Space Launch 1961

Alan B. Shepard, Jr. was the first American launched into space. His launch was quickly followed by space trips by five other astronauts. **Complete the information** about the flight of each.

Name	Date	Mission name	Duration
Shepard	5/5/61	Mercury/Redstone	15 minutes 22 seconds
Grissom	_____	_____	_____
Glenn	_____	_____	_____
Carpenter	_____	_____	_____
Schirra	_____	_____	_____
Cooper	_____	_____	_____

May 6

Spider Day

Early in May more and more spiders are seen. A fear of spiders shows a lack of knowledge about them. Use this day to **research** the common spiders listed here. **Underline** those that are poisonous.

Trapdoor spider   Wolf spider
Banded garden spider   Brown Recluse spider
Black Widow spider   Crab spider
Tarantula Green   Lynx spider
Funnel-web spider   Jumping spider
Orb Weaver spider   European Water spider

May 7

Sinking of the *Lusitania* 1915

This passenger ship sunk by German torpedoes has become one of the most famous ships in history. Below are other history-making ships. **Name** them.

1. The ship captained by Sir Frances Drake whose sailors grew so rich from looting towns that the ship was renamed. Give either name.

_____

2. Ships that brought the English settlers to Jamestown.

_____

3. The ship of mutiny captained by Henry Hudson.

_____

4. Robert Fulton's first steamboat.

_____

5. Two ironclads which fought to a draw during the Civil War.

_____

6. The first U.S. aircraft carrier.

_____

7. King Henry VIII's super-battleship of 1514.

_____

8. Two fastest British tea and wool clipper ships.

_____

9. First steamer to cross the Atlantic in 1819.

_____

10. Lord Nelson's 2000 ton sailing, wooden battleship.

_____

May 8

Birthday of Harry Truman 1884-1972

Complete the pyramid with information about Truman.

1. Middle initial   _____
2. Born in what state?   _____ _____
3. Studied what?   _____ _____ _____
4. Wife's first name   _____ _____ _____ _____
5. Bomb he authorized _____ _____ _____ _____ _____

May 9

Birthday of James M. Barrie 1860-1937

James M. Barrie is the author of *Peter Pan*, the boy who did not want to grow up. He lived in Never-Never Land where exciting adventures happen every day. One character in the story is a hungry crocodile. Here is a poem about the crocodile based on a poem created by Dennis Lee called *Alligator Pie*. **Write** a poem about a crocodile who has over eaten.

Crocodile cake
Crocodile cake
Give it to me now
Or my heart will break.
Take away my burger, take away my shake
But give it to me now, my crocodile cake.

May 10

Driving of the Golden Spike 1869

This first transcontinental railroad in the United States became a reality on this date marking the junction of the Central Pacific and Union Pacific Lines. There are many red letter dates in railroad history. Place the number of each listed on the **time line** below.

1. First sleeping car
2. First railway mail service
3. Transcontinental route
4. First efficient steam engine
5. First 200 mile per hour run
6. Dining cars

1769   1831   1837   1863   1869   1955

May 11

First U.S. Trading Ship Leaves for China 1785

This voyage took over one year. The trade goods brought back had rarely been seen before since they originated in China. In Joan Bodger's story of Clever Lazy, a young Chinese girl is put in prison until she agrees to tell the ruler of her discoveries, including how to make gunpowder.

Unscramble these other China firsts that Clever Lazy took credit for.

1. repap   _____

2. kin   _____

3. gintnirp   _____

4. ssapomc   _____

May 12

Birthday of Florence Nightingale 1820-1910

Read about the life of this amazing woman who is known as the founder of the nursing profession. **Find out**:

1. What nursing was like in the mid 1800s.
2. How she led 38 nurses to the Crimea to nurse 500 badly wounded British soldiers.
3. Why she almost died while in the Crimea.
4. What the results of her work were.
5. If Florence Nightingale were to write a letter to nurses today, what do you think she would say?

May 13

Colonists Arrive in Jamestown 1607

On this day the first permanent English settlement in America was established. These first 105 settlers were not prepared to cope with the new world. During the first seven months seventy-three died. Seven years later with the arrival of new settlers and the discovery of a crop that could be sold for profit, Jamestown, Virginia, became self-sufficient.

Read about the first 105 settlers. **Answer these questions**. What caused their deaths? Could any of these deaths have been prevented? Why or why not?

May 14

Lewis and Clark Begin Their Historic Journey   1804

These two explorers were the first to travel from St. Louis, Missouri, to the Pacific coast. What else can you **discover** about one of these trailblazers?

1. Name _____
2. Date of birth _____
3. Married _____
4. Discovery _____
5. Education _____
6. Greatest wish _____
7. Greatest fear _____

May 15

Birthday of L. Frank Baum 1856-1919

The first *Oz* book by this author led to an entire series about characters who have become familiar to us from *The Wonderful Wizard of Oz*.

Choose one *Oz* character from list one. **Write a letter** from that character to one fantasy character in list two. Your letter should reveal information about both characters.

List One	List Two
Dorothy	Mary Poppins
Cowardly Lion	Captain Hook
Tinman	Peter Pan
Scarecrow	Alice in Wonderland

May 16

First Academy Awards 1929

Academy Award Trivia **Quiz**

1. What two actors won the Best Actor award twice?

_____

2. How many actresses have won the award twice? _____

3. What sisters each won the Best Actress award?

_____

4. What actress won the award three times?

_____

5. The Barrymores were known as a great acting family. Did any ever win the award?

_____

6. What two actresses tied for the Best Actress award?

_____

May 17

Reaper Patented 1803

The reaper could do the work of six men in half the time. Many fieldhands were unhappy about its use since their jobs were no longer needed.

   1. Name an invention that has replaced people in their jobs._____

   2. Name an invention that has created many new jobs._____

Write a help wanted ad for a future job. Base your ad on fact. Possibilities might include a sea harvester, moon miner or peace analyst.

May 18

Mt. St. Helens Erupts 1980

David A. Johnston, a young scientist, was killed while studying this eruption. This was the first time this volcano had become active since 1857.

List the 3 types of volcanoes. What makes them different? Prepare a **chart** showing the differences.

Mark a map of the United States showing the location of volcanoes in this country.

Are volcanoes helpful in any way? **Explain**.

May 19

Headline Day

Newspaper headlines try to give a lot of information in a few words. Create a **headline** to report about five of your favorite books. The headline shoud make someone want to read the book.

Here are examples.

A BLUE RIBBON FOR WILBUR (*Charlotte's Web*)

RUPERT BLACK $100 RICHER TODAY (*The Toothpaste Millionaire*)

HOLE DIGGING BOYS MISTREATED AT CAMP (*Holes*)

May 20

Alliteration Day

Authors often use *alliteration* to write good descriptions. Alliteration is the repeated use of beginning sounds in a group of words. Scott Corbett uses alliteration in the title of one of his mysteries, *The Case of the Ticklish Tooth*.

Use alliteration to describe a pain in the following:
1. Head _____
2. Heel _____
3. Eyes _____
4. Toe _____
5. Leg _____

May 21

Lindbergh Lands in Paris 1927

Charles Lindbergh made this solo flight across the Atlantic Ocean in thirty-three and one half hours. He flew more than 3,600 miles.

John Glenn was the first man to orbit the Earth in a spaceship.

Read about the lives of these two men. What advice might Lindbergh have given Glenn if he had been present at the space flight briefing? **Write a dialogue** between the two men.

What qualities does a person need to attempt a thing that has never been done before?

May 22

Birthday of Arnold Lobel

Arnold Lobel is the author of the *Frog and Toad* books. These two friends have many adventures. Choose one of the problems they encounter and **write a paragraph** telling them how to **solve the problem**.

1. What should Toad do when all the animals make fun of his bathing suit?

2. What should Toad do when Frog, who is expected, does not arrive until very late on Christmas Eve?

3. What can Frog and Toad do with many large bags of leaves?

4. How can Frog get Toad out of bed to greet spring when Toad does not want to get up?

5. Frog and Toad want to climb a mountain but they are afraid of the dangerous things they might find. What should they do?

May 23

Birthday of Scott O'Dell 1903

If you have read the book or seen the film *Island of the Blue Dolphins* you know how Scott O'Dell was able to create past worlds with vivid realism.

Try one of these O'Dell books for exciting reading. Present an oral report of the story line from the main character's point of view.

The Amethyst Ring
The adventures of Julian, a young Spanish student, who impersonates a god of the Maya and travels to the Inca empire.

The Castle in the Sea
Young wealthy Lucinda tries to improve the quality of life in Isla del Oro while fearing that someone is trying to murder her.

May 24

Brooklyn Bridge Opens 1883

This was the bridge many said could not be built. For an account of how it was done, **read** *The Brooklyn Bridge* by Judith St. George.
Match these famous bridges with their locations.

1. Golden Gate	_____	A) Detroit-Canada
2. Ambassador	_____	B) Maryland
3. Chesapeake Bay	_____	C) Harlem River-New York City
4. Rainbow	_____	D) San Francisco, California
5. Hudson	_____	E) Niagara Falls

May 25

First News Telegram Sent 1844

The first news telegram was sent to New York City from Washington D.C. and described the workings of Congress.

Read several news articles from your local paper. Choose one and **summarize** the article as a ten word **telegram**.

_____

_____

_____

May 26

Freedom Day

This is a day to reflect on the freedoms Americans enjoy. To celebrate this day, do a newspaper hunt. **Find**:

1. A picture that symbolizes freedom
2. A patriotic headline
3. An article about loss of freedom
4. An event that could take place only in a free society
5. A statement concerning freedom of speech
6. The name of someone who can do something about an injustice

May 27

Find the Difference Day

Many animals seem so closely related that it is difficult to find the differences between them.

Create a chart that shows the differences between:

Frog or Toad?

1. Frogs and toads
2. Dolphins and porpoises
3. Rats and mice
4. Rabbits and hares
5. Crocodiles and alligators
6. Moose and caribou

May 28

Good Health Day

Good health requires an understanding of how your body works. Find books about the human body and **answer these questions** yes or no.

1. _____ Your skin weighs three times as much as your brain.
2. _____ Some people grow a third set of teeth.
3. _____ Your heart beats more than 36 million times a year.
4. _____ Muscles make up more than half your body weight.
5. _____ Swallowed food takes 4-8 seconds to reach the stomach.
6. _____ Blood takes 23 seconds to make a full trip around the body.

First Whooping Crane Born in Captivity 1975

Many wild creatures like the whooping crane are endangered species. Unless they are protected they will disappear from Earth. **Identify** which of these animals are also on the endangered list. Put an X by those that are endangered.

_____kit fox   _____woodchuck

_____skunk   _____grizzly bear

_____timber wolf   _____sea otter

_____gazelle

May 30

First Automobile Accident 1896

This first accident happened in New York City and was between a car and a bicycle. The driver spent the night in jail and the cyclist suffered a broken leg.

1. **List** three leading causes of automobile accidents today.

_____

_____

_____

2. **List** the advantages and disadvantages of raising the age to obtain a driver's license to twenty-one.

May 31

Johnstown Flood 1889

This flood destroyed Johnstown, Pennsylvania, taking 2,200 lives. Since that date much effort has gone into flood control and other ways of protecting the environment. The following predictions were made in 1974 by the World Future Society. **Find out** if each prediction is now reality, soon to happen or years away.

Prediction	Reality	Soon	Years Away
1. Safe disposal of radio-active wastes			
2. Effective control of oil spills			
3. Cars no longer running on gasoline			
4. Nuclear power plants located off shore			

AN ALMANAC OF THINKING ACTIVITIES

ANSWER KEY

Many of the answers in the Almanac are students' opinions. Others require current research. The answers below represent the author's research of factual information.

SEPTEMBER
2   New fire laws passed, life insurance started, and operated pumps invented.
5   Lawmen: Hickok, Masterson, Earp, Bean, others outlaws
15 Gustav Mahler
16 A. Achieving armistice in Palestine conflict B. Founder, Lambarene Hospital in Africa C. Fought against atomic testing D. Negotiation of Viet Nam cease-fire agreement E. Efforts toward settlement of Arab-Israli conflict F. Work with the poor in India
22 Son was shy, socially crude and a failure as a diplomat
23 Orbit time 164.8 years; 8 Satellites: Axis rotation: 16.1 hours; Gases: hydrogen, hydrogen, methane
27 Republican elephant, Tammany Tiger, Santa Claus

OCTOBER
3   1898, 6, 9, 4, 19, 1917
5   First to prove a rocket works in a vacuum, to work out the mathematics of rocket action, to develop rockets equipped with propellent pumps, gyro controls
9   Lennon, explosive. McCartney, witty. Harrison, withdrawn. Starr, common sense.
10 phosphate detergents cause water pollution through over production of algae.
14 HELP
15 A) Middle Atlantic States, Florida B) South Florida, Bahamas, Louisiana C) Caribbean, Mexico D) Virginia to Louisiana E) Texas Coast
16 Born Free, Steadfast Tin Soldier, Little Engine that Could, Green Eggs and Ham
19 Earl of Sandwich
20 A) Flying trapeze B) Wild animal trainer C) Aerialist D) High wire
21 physics, chemistry, physiology (medicine), literature, peace, economics
22 All false statements A) played and composed throughout life B) married, had many friends C) Sponsored work and careers of many composers
25 Answers to all items: False
28 1) Frederic Bartholdi 2) French 3) pedestal 4) Grover Cleveland 5) Emma Lazarus 6) torch 7) copper

NOVEMBER
2   A. Trail blazed by Boone B. Captured and adopted Boone C. Boone's wife D. Boone settlement
4   Killed by Uncle Ay who married Tut's wife. He was her grandfather.
7   7'9" player, Dayton, Ohio, Walter Garrett, Lloyd Free, 2/1/73
9   Killed by an angry mob
11 1) Gavirillo Princip 2) Britain, Russia, France, Italy, United States 3) four years 4) Austria-Hungary Bulgaria, Germany, Ottoman Empire 5) Woodrow Wilson
12 A) Adolphe Sax B) Levi Strauss C) Duke of Wellington D) Captain George C. Boycott
16 A) Paul Revere B) Horse C) Patrick Henry D) Big Idea E) John Hancock
17 A) 100 B) 2 C) 6,000 D) 46 feet E) 118 feet F) 390 G) 9 H) 1859 I) 1869 Total, 10, 393
22 #3
23 1. Tom Smith 3. Bat Masterson 3. Pat Garrett 4. Allan Pinkerton 5. Judge Roy Bean 6. Arizona

DECEMBER
1   Angelina Grimke, Mary Church Terrell
2   Pointillism uses dots and dashes rather than brush strokes
3   Arteriosclerosis, hypertension
6   1. writer 2. inventor 3. statesman 4. writer 5. first automobile
9   Joe Magarac, Paul Bunyan, Febold Feboldson, John Henry, Pecos Bill, Davy Crockett